TO THE PERIL OF MY LIFE

SHEKHAR GUPTA

notionpress
.com

INDIA · SINGAPORE · MALAYSIA

Copyright © Shekhar Gupta 2025
All Rights Reserved.

ISBN
Paperback 979-8-89906-586-6
Hardcase 979-8-89984-327-3

Contents

Chapter X

Chapter-XI

Chapter-XII

Chapter XIII

Contents

Acknowledgement

"…To the Peril of My Life" is based on my memoirs written long back during my Army days. But at the same time, the book is neither written as memoirs nor as a biography. That's why the incidents reproduced in various sections of this book do not follow the chronology.

While sharing some of the interesting moments of Army life with my family members and close friends, many a time I was encouraged by them to pen down all such incidents in the form of a book. Feeling that various anecdotes may help some of the readers in one way or the other, I decided to write this book after retiring from my professional career.

All the incidents included in "….To the Peril of My Life." inspired me to do well in my professional career later, and I felt that it could be equally encouraging to many readers as well. So, first and foremost, I must acknowledge the role that a short stint in the Army played in creating a strong urge to write down the occurrences.

I would also like to acknowledge the persistent coaxing and motivation that I received from my entire family and many close friends, which made this book possible.

From a security point of view, the names of some strategic locations, outposts, Army units, and formations have been changed. At the same time, respecting the personal privacy, the names of a few persons have also been altered.

Chapter-1

"…..Even to the Peril of My Life"

"Bravery is not the absence of fear, but the ability to overcome it"

–Gen PN Thapar

Then something unexpected and bizarre happened all of a sudden.

I had stopped for a while to take a few deep breaths. Behind me, everyone had stopped as well. We were in a high-altitude area of North Kashmir on a night with several feet of snow. Most of us were sweating profusely despite the sub-zero temperature. A tiring and monotonous, yet spirited, crawl by all of us had been continuing on the soft snow for the last about seven hours.

It was already past 2130 hrs, and while inching forward in the frozen surroundings, we were negotiating a sharp curve on a narrow track. Snow-laden vertical slopes on both sides of the gorge had suddenly elongated the valley at the curve. The complete silence observed by us made the path look eerie.

With his enthusiastic crawl on several feet of soft snow, Sepoy Ram Pal was leading the patrol. I was walking right behind him. That's when we heard a rumbling sound coming from the top of the cliff to our right. I gave Ram Pal a soft touch on his leg and motioned him to cease crawling and to rise right away. Behind me, the entire patrol came to a halt, and we all stood motionless with our backs pressed against the vertical slope of the hill from the top of which the growling sound came.

Yes, it was a massive avalanche! Within seconds, we heard the dull rumble turn into a thunder, and we could see hundreds of tonnes of snow rolling down the cliff just ahead of us. The roll down continued for several seconds with a reverberating sound. In a few minutes, huge heaps of snow blocked our entire passage a few metres ahead of us.

When the roll down stopped, the narrow passage through which we were supposed to move forward on our track had turned into a gigantic snow mountain.

All fourteen of us knew that we had survived by just a whisker! Had we been a few metres ahead, the entire team would have been buried with no trace of our bodies.

The oath taken by me at the Officers' Training School (OTS) three years ago, at the time of the grant of commission as an Army Officer, suddenly flashed in my mind;

"I do swear in the name of GOD that I will bear true faith and allegiance to the Constitution of India as by the law established and that I will, as in duty bound, honestly and faithfully serve in the regular Army of the Union of India and go wherever ordered, by land, sea, or air, and that I will observe and obey the commands of the President of the Union of India and the commands of any officer set over me, even to the peril of my life."

   ◈ ◈ ◈

It had all begun on the previous evening, i.e., 5th December 1982, when all the unit officers were playing cards in the officers' mess after dinner. The location was close to the LoC in a high-altitude area in North Kashmir. After a tenure of three years near Ranchi, a so-called peace station, the battalion had shifted to this operational location about four months earlier.

Despite being a field area with hostile winters, the location was otherwise awesome. The memorable journey from Jammu, particularly through the breathtaking Kashmir valley, was equally remarkable.

After a few days of the train journey from Ranchi, the battalion had disembarked at Brahmna-Di-Bari railway station near Jammu in the first week of September 1982. The entire military and personal baggage was unloaded from the train and reloaded onto a few 3-tonne and 1-tonne trucks until late in the evening the same day.

Next morning, with a packed lunch provided to everyone, the battalion convoy embarked on a 300-kilometre road journey from Jammu to Dandipore (also called Dandipura) beyond Srinagar in the Kashmir valley. Passing through Patnitop and Ramban, our convoy crossed the Banihal tunnel in the afternoon to enter the valley.

As soon as we came out of the tunnel's north portal, we caught the first glimpse of the valley in early autumn, which was stunningly captivating. It appeared to be an entirely different world. While driving down a few hairpin bends into the valley, the golden brown shades of the saffron fields around the Kazikund area presented a breathtaking sight.

The convoy halted at Srinagar for a while for tea. It was getting dark when we left for Dandipura. It took another four hours for our convoy to reach the destination for the day.

A detachment of our advance party had already reached the area a few weeks earlier. Small detachments of the advance party were present at all the posts and locations. The group located at Dandipura had prepared dinner for the entire battalion. After a long and tiresome road journey, we enjoyed a welcome hot dinner and slept late at night, only to be up early in the morning to proceed further.

The next morning, at around 0800 hrs, our convoy left Dandipura for our new location, Ranzalwan, in the Hurez Sector. The distance from Dandipura to Ranzalwan was about 65 kilometres through a fair-weather single-lane *kutcha* road, crossing Bazdan Pass at 11672 ft above the mean sea level (MSL).

The traffic on the road was regulated so that only between 0800 hrs and 1000 hrs were vehicles allowed to start from both sides of the pass. No vehicle was permitted to leave the respective areas after 1000 hrs. The road had a double-lane patch of about three kilometres at Bazdan. That's where all the vehicles from both sides were expected to park and wait until 1300 hrs in their respective lanes.

From Bazdan, the vehicles parked on both sides moved to their respective destinations at 1300 hrs. No vehicle was allowed to cross Bazdan thereafter from either side, as the weather invariably packed up in the afternoons.

On the way to Bazdan, our convoy crossed Zagbal post at around 1030 hrs, which was around 9200 ft above the MSL. We halted there for a while for tea. After about an hour of a stiff climb, our convoy reached Bazdan Pass at around noon. We had lunch at our check –post and waited until 1300 hrs to proceed further.

It was a clear, sunny day, and the view from Bazdan was truly spectacular. One could see the magnificent view of the Zanskar ranges in the northwest and the Nanga Parbat and the Godwin-Austin peaks in the north. To the northeast, one could glimpse the upper part of the imposing Habba Khatoon peak in the Hurez Valley. Looking at the snowy mountain ranges all around, little did I know that I was to cross Bazdan on foot a few more times in the ensuing winter to witness it's real beauty under a thick cover of snow.

Even in early September, I could find some patches of snow from the previous season in shady areas of the northern slopes. With a strong breeze blowing, Bazdan was rather cold, even on a sunny day.

We were told that Bazdan remained closed for traffic from November to May due to heavy snow. In the winter months, if one were to leave the Hurez Valley, the only way was to walk the distance from Ranzalwan to Dandipura after crossing Bazdan. This was a 15 to 16-hour trek over thick snow, to be completed in one go, with three short halts at the unit posts on the way.

Our convoy left Bazdan at 1300 hrs. It was a continuous descent from there. After about two hours of slow and cautious driving, we reached Natkusu, the last check-post where we halted for about 15 minutes and had a refreshing cup of tea. After about four kilometres of steep descent from Natkusu, the last 14 kilometres of the road had a gradual slope through a narrow gorge, with a *nala* flowing alongside.

As we approached our new location, the sun was about to set. Our new battalion HQ was near Ranzalwan, a small and beautiful village on the banks of the river Ramganga, flowing from Hurez to Pakistan-Occupied Kashmir (POK) in the westward direction. Ranzalwan was about 10 kilometres east of the Line of Control (LoC). The exact location of our battalion

HQ was on an open plateau after an ascent of about 2 kilometres from Ranzalwan village at an altitude of around 8800 ft.

It was almost dark when we began to unpack. All the rooms and barracks were underground with some camouflage cover on top. Later in the evening, all the officers met in the mess at around 2100 hrs for dinner. That area was not electrified in those days, and the battalion was provided with a couple of large diesel generating (DG) sets to keep the HQs lighted at night.

The officers' mess was in a wooden building, but its interiors were beautifully maintained. Soon after, I hit the bed after another long and tiring day, though the bed was nothing more than a cosy sleeping bag kept on a raised platform in an underground bunker.

The next day was designated as admin day for everyone to unpack and organise. The morning was bright and sunny, and the beauty of the place seemed even more fascinating. The plateau on which the battalion HQs were located was an oval-shaped, flattish piece of land surrounded by tall, lanky pine and willow trees. The snow-clad, high, and steep mountains on all sides added to the bewitching beauty of the valley.

The mean altitude of the Hurez Valley was around 8200 feet above the MSL. The valley offered an incredibly picturesque view as the river Ramganga meandered dashingly along through rich meadows covered with beautiful alpine, walnut, and willow trees.

In the battalion area, we had a hockey field in one corner, which was also used as a helipad during winter. In the other corner were the battalion stores, where diesel, petrol, and kerosene were stored among other provisions. The ammunition store and the battalion Kote (Keeper of Technical Equipment) were in the third and more secure corner towards the hillside.

The underground barracks for the *Jawans* were everywhere. In the central part of the plateau, two wooden buildings housed the mess for JCOs on one side and the officers' mess on the other. Right opposite the mess buildings were the office and the quarter guard buildings.

Two rifle companies were deployed on the forward posts manning the LoC along the high mountain features to the north. The remaining two companies, along with the support and admin companies, were based at the battalion HQs.

The following days, Alfa and Charlie Companies began moving to the forward positions. I was officiating as Delta company commander, and my company was kept as a reserve at the HQ. An additional responsibility of the position of Adjutant was also assigned to me.

A typical day at the battalion HQs would start with PT, followed by breakfast. Thereafter, everyone moved to their respective offices for routine work, followed by lunch in the officers' mess. After lunch, the officers would usually spend their spare time playing Bridge. Organised games would take place at 1530 hrs, and sports like hockey, football, or basketball were organised where everyone, including all the officers, would play with the troops for about one hour.

The battalion's base camp was at Dandipura, and the officer in charge there would send fresh supplies, newspapers, and incoming *Dak* to the HQ every alternate day in an administrative vehicle that went up and down for this purpose.

There were seven forward posts on the LoC, manned by two companies. Four forward posts, namely Piku, Riku, Ashok, and Anthony, were held by the Alfa Company. The Charlie Company manned three other posts, namely Bhim, Kant, and Raka. In addition, some additional operational duties were also assigned to the Charlie Company at the battalion HQ.

All the pickets involved 5 to 7 hours of climbing from the HQs. Extreme winter conditions prevailed during most of the year. The posts remained covered with snow for 7 to 8 months in a year, while Ranzalwan received snow from October to April every season.

On the forward posts, electric lamps were used for lighting purposes, for which rechargeable DC batteries were provided. Several spare batteries were recharged at the HQ, and they were periodically replaced with the discharged ones. If the replenishment of charged batteries was delayed due to a longer spell of bad weather, the backup of kerosene lamps was available. Kerosene *bukharis* were used to keep all the bunkers warm throughout the year, for which a sufficient quantity of kerosene was kept stocked.

Stocking the provisions for the winter involved a lot of administrative effort. Periodic replacement of the discharged batteries and the continued supply of tinned food items to all the forward posts was a herculean task for the battalion quartermaster.

To maintain adequate supplies of all essential commodities at the border outposts, the battalion was permitted to hire around 100 local porters and about 30 ponies throughout the year. The labour and ponies were provided by a local labour contractor named Khalil Mohammed. Khalil was the only local person with whom we could communicate, as for security reasons, Ranzalwan village and its residents were out of bounds for all ranks.

By the third week of October, Hurez Valley experienced its first heavy snowfall, about two feet. Five feet of snowfall was reported at Bazdan Pass, resulting in its official closure for vehicular traffic for that season.

The Task

On the evening of 4th December, it had been snowing intermittently since morning and several feet of snow had accumulated all around. We were about to retire to our respective bunkers after dinner when the duty clerk brought two logged wireless messages to me. The first one was from the brigade HQ, informing that 12 Jawans of the 116th battalion of the BSF returning from leave had started on foot from

Dandipura that morning and were expected to reach our location late in the evening.

The second message was from the Natkusu post, informing us that the BSF men returning from leave were to leave the Natkusu post at around 2300 hours, expecting to reach our location late and stay there for the night. As the unit's Adjutant, I was required to organise the night stay and breakfast for them. Such messages were routine, as the troops located at Hurez would invariably halt at our location during their return journey from Dandipura before moving on to Hurez the next morning.

I informed the CO about the messages before issuing telephonic instructions to the concerned persons to make the required arrangements. The CO asked me to inform him as soon as the BSF party reached our location. We all retired to our respective bunkers at around 2200 hrs. I asked the duty officer to let me know when the BSF group arrived. But throughout the night, neither the duty officer nor the duty clerk in the control room provided any information about the arrival of the BSF *Jawans*.

Heavy snowfall continued throughout the night. Early the next morning, before heading for PT, I again inquired about the BSF men from the control room, only to be informed that the party had not reached our location. We tried to contact the missing BSF men directly on their wireless set, but could not. Presumably, the battery of their wireless set had been discharged. I then asked the duty officer to send a wireless radio message to the BSF battalion, inquiring whether the party had reached Hurez directly.

I went to the PT ground and, along with others, played rugby on the fresh snow, which had risen to several feet. The Commanding Officer missed the PT that day, owing to a mild fever. I met him at the breakfast table and informed him that the leave party of the BSF personnel had not been reported to our location till then. I also informed him about the log message sent to the BSF battalion. The CO asked me to keep him posted as and when any confirmation message was received from the BSF.

At around 1100 hrs, I received a wireless message from the BSF battalion stating that the missing personnel had not reached Hurez. Another message was received from the brigade HQ, requiring us to send a rescue-cum-search patrol to look for the missing personnel. I informed Colonel Mehra, who immediately summoned all the officers to his office.

He apprised everyone of the seriousness of the issue. The CO also informed that the Brigade Commander had asked the battalion to send a search and rescue patrol towards Natkusu to look for missing BSF personnel, as they were apparently stuck somewhere between Natkusu and Ranzalwan.

We experienced the disappearance of a leave party for the first time, and everyone wondered why and how they did not reach Ranzalwan. Did they get buried under a snow avalanche?

Or did they erroneously stray into enemy territory? No one was too sure.

Even if they were stuck en route, their health was a grave concern, as the *Jawns* had been out in the open under hostile weather conditions for more than 18 hours. The missing personnel were without adequate winter clothing, as they were returning from leave. Furthermore, they were all without food after leaving Natkusu the previous night.

As per the orders from the CO, I immediately sent a search patrol of 10 selected boys with a radio set, led by an energetic JCO, *Subedar* Deep Ram, to proceed towards Natkusu along with a few porters to look for the missing BSF personnel.

Soon, the search patrol left. However, the porters, who were all local and mostly from Ranzalwan village, refused to accompany the patrol, arguing that entering the avalanche-prone track during the day may prove suicidal. *"After a fresh snowfall, entering this area during the day is like going into the jaws of a ferocious tiger,"* they reportedly said, describing the hazard along the highly avalanche-prone vertical slopes on both sides of the track to Natkusu.

After a couple of hours, the duty officer informed me that the rescue patrol could not make much headway due to heavy ground snow. I immediately informed the CO, and all officers came out of their offices to a vantage point nearby from where the patrol could be seen.

In the haze of falling snow, we could see the search patrol in the *nala* below us, struggling to proceed ahead in the heaps of fresh snow. Their modus operandi to negotiate the soft snow was that one person in the lead was trampling the snow with their feet to take one step forward, trampling again for some time to move another step.

This time-consuming method of making headway in soft snow was the reason for painfully slow progress. I spoke to *Subedar* Deep Ram over the radio, who informed me that his team was unable to make much progress due to excessive soft snow.

With that speed, it was obviously impossible to search the entire route up to Natkusu within a reasonable timeframe. We all went back to the office to consider the alternatives. The best option to locate the missing soldiers was, of course, the aerial reconnaissance of the area. But with the kind of weather and extremely poor visibility, a search operation by requisitioning a chopper had to be ruled out.

After discussing the limited options available, the consensus was to appoint one young officer to lead the patrol to ensure that the forward movement was faster and the search and rescue operation was completed quickly.

I volunteered to lead the patrol. A young Army Medical Corps (AMC) officer, Dr. (Captain) JS Walia, who was the regimental medical officer (RMO) with the unit, also offered to accompany, stating that in extreme cold weather, some of the missing personnel might require immediate medical attention.

In the next half an hour, we prepared ourselves for the task, dressed up in complete winter battle dress and carried our carbines with some ammunition. Captain Walia carried some medicines required for first aid.

I asked for a few thermoses full of hot tea and a few cookies and took two more spirited *Sepoys* with me. *Subedar* Deep Ram was informed over the radio set that we were joining the patrol. At about 1430 hrs, after a quick lunch, we all left the battalion area to catch up with the search patrol.

Within minutes, we joined the patrol. It was still snowing heavily. I took a few minutes to brief them, informing everyone that many of the missing personnel were without proper snow clothing and had not eaten any meal after their lunch at Bazdan on the previous day. I thus emphasised that our task was to safely extricate all the missing BSF personnel as soon as possible.

I also cautioned the entire patrol not to make any unnecessary sounds, as the heavy fresh snow on the vertical slopes on both sides; any sound could trigger an avalanche in the highly avalanche-prone area that we were to walk through.

Though most of the personnel seemed well motivated for the task, one of the soldiers from Bravo Company, *Sepoy* Mulk Raj, asked me why the local porters refused to accompany them. I took some time to explain to him that the porters were civilians and not soldiers like us and were working for wages, not for protecting their motherland.

I also explained to Mulk Raj that the risk to life was everywhere – while driving, running, cycling, or carrying out any other day-to-day activity. It was also explained that we were out for a noble cause of saving the lives of our fellow soldiers and the God Almighty would certainly help us to succeed. Finally, I gave Mulk Raj the option that if he still had doubts, he was most welcome to get back to the battalion HQ. But he emphatically refused and stated that he was eager to be a part of the patrol.

By the time we regrouped to begin afresh at around 15:15 hrs, the visibility had dropped considerably, with the snowfall continuing unabated. By then, everyone was clear that speed was of utmost importance to prevent the BSF men from freezing or starving to death. *Sepoy* Hem Raj of Delta Company was given the responsibility to be in the lead, and I was right behind him.

Once again, Hem Raj began the task of making a track in the snow by trampling it step by step. In a loud whisper, I ordered Hem Raj to start crawling on the snow as rapidly as he could so that the rest of the patrol could walk over the hardened track made by his crawl. My instruction apparently left Hem Raj flabbergasted as he immediately stopped and turned to me.

Without any intention to disobey my instructions, Hem Raj was certainly not convinced.

"If I crawl Sa'ab, I may sink in the soft snow and fall into the rivulet flowing just below us," he politely whispered back to me. I tried to explain that there was no danger of sinking deep into the soft snow while crawling, as the weight of the body would evenly spread over a larger surface area. But he did not seem to comprehend the logic and looked reluctant. I then asked him to fall back behind me.

I decided to take the lead and started crawling myself. Though crawling in soft snow was quite tough, it was way faster than trampling the snow for every step forward. Hem Raj continued looking at me curiously while walking on the track made by the trail of my crawl. Dr (Captain) Walia, *Subedar* Deep Ram and all others followed him.

That was my first experience crawling on fresh snow, and it turned out to be tougher than I had imagined. I had to exercise my arms and legs vigorously as if I were swimming, but displacing the soft snow was certainly far more tiring than swimming.

After a while, realising that it was a faster way to move forward with no risk of getting sunk in soft snow, Hem Raj quickly moved ahead, tapped on my back, and indicated that he wanted to take his turn to lead. Already running out of breath, I too needed some time to recoup my energy. So, I handed over the lead to him. Looking backwards, it gave me satisfaction that we had covered a distance of about 40 metres within a few minutes of my crawl!

From that moment onwards, there seemed to be a sort of competition within the entire patrol to take the lead. *Subedar* Deep Ram was the next to come forward. Normally, the RMOs did not take part in any such missions, nor were they required to do so. After a while, I was pleasantly surprised when Dr (Captain) Walia volunteered to lead.

Dr (Captain) Walia amply exhibited his physical fitness, which would match any infantry officer's. He took the lead several times and crawled swiftly with his lean and fit body frame. His regimental spirit and sense of commitment were admirable and exemplary.

We had to search the entire 14-kilometre track from our battalion location to Natkusu. It took us about 40 minutes to cover the first kilometre, and the progress became a bit faster thereafter. By then, the snowfall had become intermittent, and we continued progressing steadily. The temperature had dropped further, but most of us were sweating with intense crawling. By the time it was dark, we had covered slightly more than two kilometres towards Natkusu.

By 19:00 hrs, it stopped snowing, and the sky cleared. This caused the temperature to dip several notches further. By then, the crawl in the snow had started to take its toll on our energy levels. But everyone was too motivated to be bogged down.

With a gradual climb on our way, we had gained about 300 metres in altitude during our advance. The amount of ground snow distinctly increased with every step. By 2100 hrs, we had covered more than half the distance, but we could not find our subjects, which was a bit concerning.

❧ ❧ ❧

We were lucky to have escaped the deadly avalanche. A huge snow stack suddenly blocked our way in front, and I looked at my men; their morale seemed to have nosedived, reflecting the shadow of death clearly on their faces.

The soldier right behind me suggested that we'd better turn back and return to Ranzalwan, as it seemed virtually impossible to cross the formidable dumps of snow obstructing our way. He apprehended that we could encounter another avalanche ahead and might not be as lucky next time.

That was the time to act as the leader of the team once again. I explained to the entire team that we were on a noble mission to save the lives of some innocent fellow soldiers. I also emphasised that God helped us safely reach that far, despite a massive killer avalanche landing a few metres ahead. I also reminded my soldiers that we were out to provide succour to a few fellow soldiers who were still lost in extremely cold weather without food, adequate snow clothing, or medicines and desperately needed rescue.

Captain Walia and *Subedar* Deep Ram also joined me in convincing the team. Everyone appeared to agree with the argument that if we were to die, we would have been killed by the avalanche a little while ago. It took some time for the entire stock to get fully motivated to start afresh.

I then turned my attention towards the colossal heap of snow facing us and took the lead by crawling upwards. The amount of snow was so great that initially, I had to use both crawling and trampling techniques. The patrol party watched me endure a formidable crawl through the enormous mound of snow. After a while, Dr Walia took over from me, followed by *Subedar* Deep Ram.

The progress was painfully slow, as it took us about half an hour to move a few metres upwards. The climb over the snow mountain was more daunting than I had initially thought. We continued by taking short turns, as our energy levels had decreased considerably by then.

The sky was clear by then, causing the temperature to dip further. After toiling hard for about three hours, we found ourselves on the other side of the mound. It was the time when most of us were famished and had to curb a strong urge to eat something, as the laborious climb sapped up the leftover energy of our bodies during the past three hours or so.

The tougher climb was over, and going down was way easier. But before beginning the crawl downwards, we celebrated our minor success with some tea and cookies. We opened one of the three flasks, and poured tea into an enamel mug. All of us had a couple of sips with a cookie each. Feeling re-energised by the refreshment, we resumed our forward movement before the warmth of our bodies cooled down.

We had moved about a kilometre ahead after crossing the avalanche when *Sepoy* Hem Raj, who was crawling in front, was suddenly stopped by *Subedar* Deep Ram behind him. Deep Ram then gestured to everyone to stop. We could hear some hushed and unclear sounds ahead of us. I immediately moved forward and joined Deep Ram. Yes, there were some distinct sounds—not animals, for sure. Had we closed in on the missing BSF personnel, or was it an enemy patrol?

I gestured to Hem Raj to keep moving. *Subedar* Deep Ram and I also inched forward behind him. As I drew closer, I saw a darkish cavity about twenty metres ahead, on the slope to our right from where the whispering sounds emanated. I signalled to two of my men to take a position on the ground to cover our movement, and I, along with Deep Ram, cautiously moved ahead. The whispers had become audible by then.

"Dogras?" There came a forced whisper. The sound seemed to originate from the dark cavity, which was a natural cave formed inside the hill. "We are from the BSF."

Hearing this, *Sepoy* Hem Raj, crawling in front, got up, turned back, and whispered to me, "Sa'ab, we have caught up!" I still remember his beaming face and the glitter in his eyes. The entire patrol was overjoyed, but we were careful not to make any sounds. I reached the cave and peeped inside. Yes, all the 12 BSF men were huddled up against each other.

Deep Ram also came forward to join me. As we approached them, the leader of the BSF party, *Havaldar* Matadeen came forward and tried to touch my feet with his shivering hands, but I stopped him.

"Sir, the Dogras have saved us," he said, as tears of gratitude flowed from his eyes.

We offered them tea and a couple of cookies each. Dr (Captain) Walia quickly swung into action, examined all of them, and gave them first aid medicines like Crocin and Ibuprofen.

Matadeen informed me that after they left Natkusu on their way to Ranzalwan, it started snowing heavily, and the visibility fell to almost zero. Since many of them were returning from annual leave without snow boots and snow *parkas*, they decided to wait in the cave for the snowfall to stop and visibility to improve.

Matadeen told us that they waited the whole night, but heavy snowfall continued unabated. By the morning, things went from bad to worse, and they found several feet of snow piled up all around. Matadeen further said that in the morning, four of his men were running a high temperature, and five others suffered from frostbite on their toes. As nine members of his group were not in a position to walk on their own and, the remaining three, including Matadeen, were also too weak to walk the distance, they decided to wait for help.

As it continued snowing heavily throughout the next day, they decided to stay put together in the cave's shelter, knowing well that sooner or later, a patrol from the nearby unit of Dogras would certainly come to their rescue.

Although our fatigue appeared to have evaporated after achieving the elusive success, we rested for a while in the cave. Soon, we reorganised ourselves and prepared for our return journey.

When we started walking on our return trek, it was quarter past two at night. Our return journey offered a different challenge. Nine BSF constables and their weapons had to be carried back. Following a roster, we carried the ailing *Jawans* for 10-12 minutes each. Meanwhile, the message of catching up with the BSF men was conveyed to the battalion HQs over the wireless set.

Once again, we had to negotiate the mountain of snow formed by the avalanche. Despite a foot track already formed, with extra load on our shoulders, it tested our endurance again. But once we crossed it, the going seemed easier.

Except for the additional load on our shoulders, our walk back to the unit HQs on a downward slope seemed quicker and easier. Our onward movement had formed a walking track on the soft snow. A drop in temperature had hardened the snow on our path, making our movement swifter, and the risk of an avalanche was also minimal.

Taking all the BSF men along, it took us about five hours to walk back to our battalion location. At about 0730 hrs, we entered the battalion area. To my utter surprise, the CO and all officers at the HQ, who had monitored the progress of our onward movement earlier, were awake throughout the night waiting for our return. In addition, there were about 50 more battalion personnel who all cheered us on as we reached.

A JCO with a few men carried and escorted the BSF men to a makeshift hospital in the barracks, which had been warmed up to a comfortable temperature. Matadeen and his team were then subjected to a detailed examination by the RMO, Dr (Captain) Walia. A hot breakfast was served to them, and the medical detachment administered the required medication.

After a day of rest at our location, five BSF men who had suffered from frostbite were evacuated to the Command Hospital Udhampur by two helicopter sorties. The remaining men were kept at our location for three more days. On the fourth day, before they were escorted to their battalion location at Hurez, *Havaldar* Matadeen came to me and thanked me again for the rescue.

It was hard to explain to him that it was a part of our duty, more as fellow human beings than anything else. Later, due to recognition of our act, the President of India and the Chief of the Army Staff decorated a few of us with gallantry awards.

Even after so many years, I vividly remember the finer details of the incident. The adverse conditions under which the rescue operation was conducted are the reasons this memory stays with me. The incident once again instilled in me a belief that if one has the resolve and passion to achieve something, nothing can stop one from doing so.

The Army experience, in addition to training its officers in many other attributes, specifically equips them with self-confidence and decision-making skills under adverse conditions. There is no doubt that fear is among the strongest human emotions. In addition to physical fear, the fear of the unknown can sometimes overpower our minds. Self-confidence, honesty of purpose, and bold decision-making are the keys to overcoming all kinds of fears.

Chapter-II

When The Going Gets Tough...

'Quartered in snow, silent to remain; when the bugle calls, they shall rise and march again.'
—A famous quote about the military forces.

Then came the testing moment. I heard the instructor, Captain Rathi, order loudly, "Commando Shekhar Gupta."

I stepped out to take my turn and after a signal from the instructor, dived into the pool, swam up to the iron stand and slowly, but steadily climbed about 25 metres up the vertical holds of steel using my arms and legs. I was trying to concentrate on commencing the most challenging 30-metre walk of my life.

On reaching the top, I stood firm on a 14-inch-wide plank. Using a towel tied up on an iron hook on the stand above me, I cleaned the residual water from my head and face. I could see the entire Belgaum town from that elevation. The speed of the wind on the top was strong enough to shake one's confidence at a height of over 80 feet on a narrow plank without any side support or protection. I focused on the job before signalling my readiness to the instructor waiting on the poolside.

'Yes, Shekhar, you can do it, *' I whispered to myself*

"Commando Shekhar, walk," shouted Captain Rathi after getting the 'ready' signal from me.

I took a deep breath. Making a conscious effort not to look below, I started walking on the narrow bridge formed by the plank, ensuring that my mind's uncertainty was not reflected in my gait. The strong breeze shook everything, including the plank, my body, and my confidence. Suddenly, a slogan written all over the boundary walls in the Infantry School flashed in my mind:

'When the going gets tough, the tough get going.'

Soon, I had walked half the distance over the plank confidently, but then found myself gaping at yet another tough task. In the middle of the plank, there were six steps to climb up, a few steps to walk on the upper elevation, and then six steps again to return to the lower plank. Confidently going up six steps on the plank at a height of 25 metres with gusty winds was truly a test of nerves.

As I took the first step forward on the upper plank, it quivered vigorously. I concentrated harder, overcame the fear, and walked over the remaining part. However, after reaching the lower plank, I was more comfortable in the latter part of the walk.

As I completed the confidence walk, I realised I had performed fairly well. At that very moment, I was relieved to hear a call from the instructor, indicating that I had qualified the first part of the most dreaded test of the commando course.

However, the delight of the sweet taste of success was short-lived. I quickly shifted my focus to the next and arguably more difficult part. The stand on the other end, on which the plank rested, was higher. From the upper part of that iron stand, a thick rope was tied across to another iron stand about 20 metres apart towards the other end of the pool.

The next task was to do a monkey crawl on the rope tied between the two stands up to a red ribbon tied at a distance of 10 metres. On reaching the red ribbon, one was expected to bring both legs down and hang on the rope by holding it with both hands for a while. On getting further orders from the instructor, one was supposed to drop into the pool below by keeping both legs vertically straight, with both toes stretched and pointed downwards towards the pool.

I was trying to mentally prepare myself for the task when Captain Rathi signalled me to begin. I turned my back to the direction I was supposed to move, grabbed the rope above me, hung on to it with both hands, slowly pulled both my legs up, and crossed my ankles over the rope. After waiting to stabilise for a few seconds, I began 'monkey crawling' towards the red ribbon with coordinated strokes of my arms and legs.

Considering that my movements were on a rope tied across at a height of about 28 metres, there was no scope for any slip-up. I 'monkey crawled' steadily backwards up to the red mark on the rope, where I stopped and gradually brought my legs down. Holding the rope firmly with both my hands, I took a few deep breaths and waited for a while to get my body balanced.

A loose hold of the rope or a faulty jump from this height could result in a serious injury, even though there was 25 feet deep water in the pool below. The monkey crawl had drained my body of all its leftover energy, and a few seconds' pause there seemed eternal.

"Commando Shekhar ready to jump, sir," I announced loudly after attaining my body balance.

'The defining moment has come. *' I told myself.*

"Commando Shekhar... jump," Captain Rathi shouted from the poolside.

ॐ ॐ ॐ

Being an infantry officer, the commando course was compulsory for me. It was required to be completed as one of the three legs of the Young Officers' (YOs') Course. After about five months of my commissioning into the 27th Battalion of the Dogra Regiment, I, along with Lieutenant Rajeev Sapra, was nominated for my first in-service training programme by the Army HQ.

The YOs' course at Infantry School, Belgaum, had three legs. The first was the tactics leg, which lasted about six weeks. This was followed by a six-week platoon weapons training course and finally, five tough weeks of the commando leg, also known as the commando course.

At Infantry School, Belgaum, as per the regulations in force, for internal commuting during training hours, we were allowed to ride only the bicycles provided to us. Lieutenant Rakesh, my friend who was one batch senior to me in OTS, was also there to undergo the YOs' course with me. In contrast, Lieutenant Jatish Sharma, another friend and senior, was already undergoing the previous YOs' course and was in the next leg of the YOs' at the Infantry School.

Jatish did very well in both weapons and tactics legs and not only got an instructor's grade (also called I-Grade) but was also awarded the 'commando dagger', a distinct honour meant for the topper of the course.

After 12 weeks, the first two legs ended. A few of us planned a short trip to Goa, which we thoroughly enjoyed. As we returned to Belgaum after the vacation, the preparation for the commando course started playing on my mind. I prepared myself mentally for the rigorous 5 weeks of commando training ahead. I took the mandatory haircut, requiring all the trainee officers to get their heads clean-shaven and prepared 3 sets of my olive green *Dangri* (overalls) that we were required to wear during the training.

The forenoon of the first day of the course involved an introduction to the course, our grouping into platoons, and certain basic information. The entire course strength was divided into a few platoons, and within a platoon, the commandos were supposed to work in buddy pairs (also called buddies) during the entire duration of the course.

Buddy pairs were formed randomly, but an effort was made to have both buddies with approximately the same height and weight. My batch-mate, Lieutenant Subhash Sen (retired as Brigadier), was chosen to be my buddy. As a departure from normal practice, all the officers undergoing commando training were required to remove the rank epaulettes from their shoulders. Furthermore, the trainee officers were addressed by prefixing the word 'commando' before their names instead of their respective ranks.

The initial few days of the training reminded me of the opening address by the commando wing in charge, a Lieutenant Colonel rank officer, in which he had informed us that the Indian Army's commando course was considered among the toughest in the world. That statement was to prove more than true during the ensuing five-week period. The commando course lived up to its reputation of being extremely tough, requiring top physical fitness and mental robustness to complete it successfully.

The course did not strive to turn the trainees into superhumans within five weeks. The objective, however, was to make us realise the super and latent capabilities of the human body and mind to endure, which most of us had not realised earlier. Furthermore, various tough tests to be passed during the course were expected to give us the confidence for life to overcome any adverse situation requiring extreme physical and mental fortitude.

The daily routine during the course would commence at around 0400 hrs with a mug of hot tea and preparations for two tough sessions of physical training (PT) beginning at 0500 hrs and lasting two hours. For most of the time during the PT period, the buddies would carry each other by turns. Thereafter, following a brief bathing and breakfast break, we were supposed to undertake a couple of sessions of learning unarmed combat (UAC).

UAC mostly involved physical exercises in a sandpit, including 'double-decker' push-ups with the buddy on top, front rolls, back rolls, side rolls, and running by lifting one's buddy in one way or another. The aim was to prepare us physically for the actual hand-to-hand fight. It was only in the last about 15 minutes of the two-hour sessions for UAC that the *ustads* taught us the actual unarmed combat to be practised with our respective buddies.

The next two hours of the day normally involved strenuous obstacle training, with the first hour dedicated only to 'toning up' our bodies, which involved short sprints, numerous push-ups, rope climbing, sit-ups, and pull-ups at a high beam.

After a welcome lunch break, the afternoon training involved 2-3 hours in commando tactics like raids and ambushes, followed by the evening routine comprising UAC, obstacle course, tactics classes, map reading exercises, etc. Training sessions generally continued up to 1800 hrs in the evening, with a 15-minute tea break at 1600 hrs.

The latter part of the evening would generally involve a training film on a commando training subject like raid and ambush. On some days, instead of the training film, there would be practical training on sentry silencing and moving stealthily in the enemy area at night.

Training sessions generally ended at around 19:30 hrs, giving us a brief bathing break before dinner. We eagerly waited for all the meals during the day as the strenuous routine would leave us starving hours before the scheduled time. After dinner, the lights were out at 21:30 hrs daily.

In addition to the above routine, there were a few special tests and exercises which were expected to be completed successfully. Five forced marches were 8, 16, 24, 32, and 40 kilometres. During the said forced marches, a trainee was supposed to carry a large backpack filled with sand weighing 24 kilograms and a 7.62 MM SLR rifle in the battle order with heavy ammo boots on. The timings to qualify were such that one had to virtually jog through the whole length of the marches.

Then there were a couple of map-reading tests for which the trainee commandos would be sent into a thick forest in buddy pairs and were expected to do the map reading through the forest. With the help of the compass, they were expected to reach together at a given point on the other side of the forest after covering the given distance.

Towards the end of the course, there was an exercise called 'Survival' in which the commandos in buddy pairs were supposed to live off the land inside a thick forest for 48 hours without food or water. The buddy pairs were sent into the forest to reach a point on the other side of the forest by covering about 45 kilometres with the help of area maps and a compass. Towards the end of the forest, a river in spate with a span of about 80 metres needed to be crossed by holding a low-hanging thick rope.

Last but certainly not least, was the final test, which included a confidence walk and a commando jump. This test was considered to be the toughest and was conducted on the penultimate day of the course. There was a big water pool, about 50 metres long, about 20 metres wide, and about 8 metres deep. In between the pool, three high iron stands were erected.

The first two stands were approximately 25 metres apart and linked by a 14-inch-wide plank, which made a sort of bridge between them. In between, the plank was raised by about two metres, with climbing and descending steps on both sides. The second stand was a bit higher and linked with a thick rope tied across to the third and last iron stand of the same height.

The next part of the test, called the "confidence walk," involved climbing up the first stand to reach the plank and walking across the plank to reach the other end. Any hesitation by any commando in walking on the plank or climbing up or down the stairs of the mid-plank would require him to repeat the test by returning to the point from where he had started. In case anyone showed any lack of confidence in the second attempt also, one would be dubbed a failure, only to undergo the entire training course again at a later date.

The final act required the commandos to hold the rope, move towards the last stand by monkey crawling, stop at a designated point in the middle of the rope, hang onto the rope with both arms straightened, and wait for the instructions to 'jump' by dropping down into the pool. Not executing the jump correctly would result in failure in the course.

To complete the course successfully, one was also expected to pass a few tough PT tests, the UAC, a grenade launching test, several map-reading exercises & tests, some written papers, quite a few practical exercises on commando operations, and a time-bound obstacle course test.

At times, the course appeared to be tougher than expected. Every trainee was thus watchful and keen to ensure they completed every test successfully without any hitch, as no one wanted to come back to undergo the same ordeal.

At the end of a typical day, we would be dead tired and fast asleep immediately on hitting the bed at 21:30 hrs. Notwithstanding a rigorous pre-course training for several weeks, the muscles of my entire body badly ached during the first week of training. However, after the 8-kilometre forced march at the end of the first week, the body seemed to be toned up.

The 8-kilometre forced march was required to be completed in one hour and five minutes. That meant that one had to literally jog through the entire distance. Jogging for over an hour in battle dress with ammo boots and carrying a 24-kilogram sandbag inside the backpack and a rifle was not easy. The initial one kilometre seemed like an unending pain. But after that, once the body warmed up, it seemed just like going through mechanical motions. In the end, like most of the other commandos, I could easily qualify for the first forced march. What worried me were the ensuing 32 and 40-kilometre forced marches towards the end of the course.

Days of training passed, and I would tick off every passing day of the course on a calendar, counting the remaining days almost daily. The 16 and 24-kilometre route marches also came to an end, though the latter troubled me a bit towards the end. By that time, the body seemed to have adapted to the strenuous routine, and occasionally, one would feel loads of energy and strength.

Towards the end of the fourth week, I stared at the impending 32-kilometre forced march. By that time, I, along with most of the commandos, had passed all the other tests that were conducted.

The day came when I found myself marching 32 kilometres with a heavy backpack on my shoulders. Even after four weeks of rigorous training with a rich diet provided in the mess, achieving the milestone in less than four hours and twenty minutes seemed quite an uphill task. While jogging through the distance, the best motivation was to continue reminding oneself that one would never come back to Belgaum to undergo the commando course all over again.

However, there were a few unlucky ones. Despite being in the best physical shape and having optimum preparations, a few trainees either had a fracture, a twisted ankle, or some kind of bacterial infection during the training. Those unfortunate ones were sent back to their respective units in between, only to start their preparations for undergoing some future commando course .

The Survival

Finally, the course reached the last and most eventful week. It began with a survival exercise. We were all left in a thick forest called Jamboti Reserve Forest. The forest was so dense and difficult to negotiate that I still have vivid memories of surviving through it even after more than four decades.

Located in the Jamboti hills in Karnataka, the forest is a 'mosaic of the tropical and sub-tropical moist broadleaf forest', rich in wildlife including leopards, gaur, spotted deer, cheetals, sambars, foxes, sloth bears, wild dogs, king cobras and a few threatened species of mammals, birds and reptiles. So rich is the wildlife and flora & fauna in the forest that later in 2011, it was declared a wildlife sanctuary and renamed Bhimgad Wildlife Sanctuary. According to reports, this sanctuary also has elephants and tigers nowadays.

A necessary condition for completing the survival exercise successfully was that both buddies had to pass the test together. To survive for 48 hours in the dreaded forest, each buddy pair was equipped with a compass and a map of the local area.

During the initial training days, we were taught snake handling, which included catching, skinning, and making a snake edible after discarding some of its body parts. It was strictly prohibited to kill any animal or reptile for food during the exercise, but an unspoken understanding was that snakes could be killed without using the service weapons. In addition, we were also trained to make fire by friction, without a matchbox.

The trainees were allowed to carry a water bottle and a mess tin (an aluminium bowl) for cooking any edible vegetation we collected during the exercise. In addition, every commando was given a few live rounds with a service rifle for self-protection. It was clearly instructed that the live rounds, if used for hunting, could invite severe punishment, including dismissal from service.

After the buddy pairs were released into the forest for ten minutes each, each team was supposed to choose its respective route by resorting to independent map reading. Once let into the forest, all the buddy pairs were on their own for 48 hours of survival in the said forest.

When our twosome was released, it was almost noon. As we entered the forest, I took responsibility for map-reading and route selection, while my buddy Subhash assumed the duty of food collection and safety en route.

We also prepared and carried a thin Y-shaped branch for any possible snake handling in the forest. I was concentrating on my navigation job while my buddy collected some tender sprouts in his backpack for dinner. We could make good progress during the initial two hours. The map indicated a small rivulet almost halfway on our route, and we aimed to reach there before nightfall.

Initially, the terrain and vegetation did not pose any difficulty for our movement. But beyond a point, it became toilsome to move briskly. The undergrowth in the forest was so thick that at times, for several tens of metres, we had to crawl through the narrow 'tunnel'-shaped route formed by the wild animal movement through the thick growth of thorny bushes, as there was no other way to move ahead.

We recharged our water bottles from a natural source on the way. Both of us had an understanding to continue walking until we reached the rivulet. During our movement through the forest, we were fortunate to see some wildlife, including a variety of birds and fowls, a few rabbits, jackals, and wild cats.

We, however, did not encounter any dangerous animals like tigers, sloth bears, wild boars, or even hyenas. In the afternoon, hot and humid weather of June took its toll, and we felt completely dehydrated when we reached the banks of the rivulet about an hour before the last light.

The water in the rivulet appeared crystal clear, and we replenished our water bottles after drinking plenty. We then started looking for a safe place to spend the night near the rivulet. While doing so, Sen spotted a big greenish snake, apparently a non-poisonous one. We swung into action and, by putting all the teachings into practice, we killed the snake, discarded six inches from its head & tail, skinned it, cut it into small pieces with our rifle bayonet, and our preparations for cooking a non-vegetarian dish were complete!

We selected a thick Y-shaped branch of a big tree near the water body for making a *machaan* for our night rest. Sen took over the responsibility of preparing the *machaan* while I started preparations for cooking. It took a lot of effort to make fire with stones, as the surroundings were quite moist near the water body. I had to look for some dry grass and leaves from an open and seemingly sunny area, which was a few hundred metres away. It was only after that the fire could be made.

I boiled the plant sprouts with the pieces of the snake for dinner. Even without any salt, spices, or condiments, it seemed to be one of the most delicious meals we had ever eaten! Later, we came to know that not many of the buddy teams were lucky enough to have as sumptuous a dinner as we did.

While I was busy cooking, my buddy erected the *machaan* on the tree identified earlier. The bayonet of his rifle came in handy for cutting smaller branches and creepers needed to do so. The *machaan* was pretty high and looked quite safe.

We had collected a lot of firewood and could make a reasonably big fire to keep the wild animals at bay. It also provided us with some illumination.

The next morning, we were up before 0500 hrs, fresh and rejuvenated for another challenging day ahead. The second day involved covering a distance of about 20 kilometres to cross the jungle and reach a designated point. After crossing the rivulet, the movement through the forest earlier in the morning was painfully slow, as we again encountered a lot of undergrowth. Even after the undergrowth thinned out by noon, moving forward in the dense forest in the semi-mountainous terrain itself was fatiguing.

At some places, we had to squat and move on our haunches through the narrow openings in the shrubs. While doing so, we were alert to keep a watchful eye for any wild animals or poisonous snakes around us. In case of any such eventuality, we had kept our rifles loaded with live rounds, with safety catches on.

Except for some wild fruits in the forest and some tender plant sprouts, we did not find anything exciting to eat on the second day. The second day seemed far more exhausting. But by now, we had realised that the best way to get over the treacherous exercise was to take it as a 'once-in-a-lifetime adventure'.

We reached the designated area by the last light after crossing the entire forest where tented accommodation was made available. No cooked meals were, however, provided, and each buddy pair was required to cook and eat whatever 'food' they could collect from the forest.

Two of the buddy pairs had lost their way in the forest, and search parties were sent to locate and guide them to the designated place. A few very light signals were also fired into the sky to direct them to the location of the camping area. We were tired as hell and hurriedly boiled and ate the sprouts we had collected. The second night in a tent was relatively comfortable, and we fell asleep as soon as we hit the beds.

When we got up early the next morning, it was raining heavily. The exercise was to end by noon after reaching the rendezvous, which was about 14 kilometres from the camping site. At the end of the route, it required crossing a river with the support of a low-hanging thick rope tied across.

Undeterred by the torrential rain, we set off at around 0800 hrs. The rain capes we carried came in quite handy. The terrain on the third day was relatively easier to cover compared to the first two days as there was not much vegetation. After walking for about three hours, we reached the banks of the Supa River.

Due to heavy rain in the catchment area that morning, the discharge of water was precariously high, and its sight was frightening. All buddy pairs were required to cross the river in an organised manner, as per the directions of the instructors present there. Four rescue teams with rescue boats were kept ready on both sides of the river for any mishap. Two more rescue teams were in a state of readiness about two hundred metres downstream.

About two and a half feet above the river surface, a thick rope was tied across the span of the river. We were required to cross over by holding onto the rope and making sure that the rifles and ammunition that we carried were kept well above the water level.

While crossing over, I had to keep half of my body above the water to keep the weapon dry. It required keeping one's body pulled up, closer to the rope all through the span of the river, which made the task more laborious. The rain was pouring unabated, and the rapid current of the water was constantly pushing my body downstream, which further strained my arms holding the rope. The plight of my buddy behind me was no better. The buoyancy provided by the river water, however, helped us to complete the task successfully.

Crossing the river under the trying circumstances sapped the entire energy from my worn-out body, making the remaining 6-kilometre walk even more demanding. When we reached the rendezvous at around 1330 hours, it had stopped raining. We expected that a hot lunch would be served to us, but shockingly, each buddy pair was given a live chicken, and we were supposed to cook it for lunch without using any utensils. The vegetarians were given some potatoes.

I dressed down the chicken immediately while Sen made the fire. There was a lot of clay around, and we coated a thick cover of wet clay around the dressed chicken and put it over the fire. After keeping it over the flames for about an hour, the dried and hardened clay coating was removed. The chicken inside was cooked and ready to be eaten as barbecue.

Under the circumstances, the lunch we ate that afternoon was extremely satisfying. After lunch, the exercise ended, and the mechanical transport took us back to the Infantry School. Two more rigorous tests awaited us to mark the end of the final and eventful week of the memorable training course.

Last, But Not the Least

After reaching the Infantry School campus late in the evening, we rested for the night only to prepare mentally for the 40-kilometre forced march. After a day of routine training, the much-awaited day arrived. The event began at around 0800 hrs in the morning after we were served a light breakfast. It was cloudy, yet very hot and humid. The entire course, consisting of about 200 commandos, was released in buddy pairs with a 2-minute gap between each pair.

The next five hours and twenty-five minutes seemed to be unending, particularly after the tiring survival exercise that ended a couple of days earlier. Like in the shorter versions of the forced marches held earlier, after every kilometre, drinking water was made available along with a paramedic to take care of any medical emergency. Two mobile medical teams with doctors, connected via wireless radio sets, were also patrolling the entire route.

After we had covered about 12 kilometres, in a development that initially seemed to be a welcome one, it started raining heavily. At the outset, the rainwater provided a respite from the sweltering heat. After a little while, however, I realised that it was becoming increasingly harder to move ahead due to heavy rain and strong headwind on the one hand, and the increased weight of the wet sand in the backpack, on the other.

In addition to the heavier weight on the back, heavy rain turned it stiff and with every step, it started rubbing hard against my back, making the jog more troublesome. At the halfway mark, I was not sure whether under those conditions, it would be possible for me to complete the march within the given time frame.

But then, all of a sudden, the rain stopped and so did the strong winds. The dark clouds gave way to several sky-blue patches in between, and soon the going became a bit easier. Thereafter, the excitement of finishing the march in time seemed to work positively on my mind, and the body pains seemed to subside with every kilometre mark.

In the end, I, along with my buddy Sen and most of the commando trainee officers, could complete the longest of the forced marches with 'excellent' timing. That evening, our entire focus shifted to the last day of the course when the last and most feared test was to be held.

On the day of reckoning, we were taken to the location of the test immediately after lunch. Another commando platoon of our course was already undergoing the test when we reached the pool area. The sight of the commandos walking on a high plank, monkey crawling at that height, and jumping into the pool triggered anxiety in everyone's mind.

This combo test was something one could not prepare beforehand, and it was hoped that one would not only be able to walk confidently on the plank but also be able to jump from the rope as per the course requirement.

The platoon ahead of us finished the test soon, and we were signalled to move closer to the pool. The instructor, Captain Rathi, explained in detail the dos and don'ts of the test and the requirements for qualifying. I was seventh in my platoon to undergo the test, which seemed to provide some relief, as watching the earlier six commandos completing the task gave me some extra confidence that I could also do what others had already done.

❧ ❧ ❧

Hanging on a 27-metre high rope, I concentrated for a few seconds before jumping and quickly recollected the tips for a successful jump learned during the training. I straightened and joined my legs, stretched both the toes vertically downwards, and released the grip of my hands on the rope, making sure that both my arms were parallel and firmly stretched straight upwards with palms open and all fingers pointing to the sky.

The drop into the pool was seamless. As soon as my toes touched the surface of the water, I knew that I had qualified with good grades. But it seemed like hours before my feet touched the bottom of the pool softly and the float of the water started pushing me upwards. As soon as my head came out of the water, one of the rescue teams rapidly moved its safety boat towards me. By that time, I had already started swimming towards the finishing point.

The exaltation of qualifying for one of the toughest training programmes on earth was strangely elating. No doubt all the infantry officers and many chosen officers from various regiments and corps were also nominated to undergo the commando course, but by completing the training successfully, one could only prove a point to oneself.

The commando training revealed to me the strength and belief of the human mind on the one hand and the immense latent physical capabilities of the human body, on the other. This revelation remains with me for life and has helped me overcome many difficult situations in my professional and personal life.

Chapter-III

Lieutenant Sapra's Engagement

"Failure doesn't exist. It is only a change of direction."

—Alejandro Jodorowsky

I experienced a few tense moments after pressing the doorbell button, before I heard someone approaching the door. As the door opened, I found myself facing Mrs Pal.

"Good afternoon, Ma'am," I greeted her with folded hands, which she reciprocated with a smiling nod.

"Is Lieutenant Pal at home?" I enquired. I could feel my ears getting red hot with anxiety.

"I am afraid he is not. He is still in office," she replied with her usual grace and courtesy. Gesturing to usher me in, she said, "Why don't you come in, Lieutenant Shekhar?"

I hesitated for a moment. As per Army etiquette, an officer is not supposed to enter the house of another officer in his absence. Furthermore, I was returning from games wearing a T-shirt and shorts, which was not a 'proper' dress to call on a brother officer in his absence.

I hesitated for a second and thought of returning. But then I was reminded of my confident assurance to Lieutenant Sapra. Banking on my family acquaintances with Pals, I decided to put aside the etiquette for the evening and entered the house after thanking Mrs Pal.

"Actually, I wanted to discuss something personal and important with him," I said, entering a clean and elegant living room. "I think I can wait for a while for him to come back."

"Please be seated," she said, pointing towards the sofa. "Would you like a glass of water?" It was more of a statement than a question as she turned towards the kitchen and brought a glass of water.

"What would you like to have, tea or coffee?" she asked me.

"I won't mind a cup of tea, Ma'am, but only if it is not inconvenient to you," I said.

"Not at all," she said, smilingly.

As she went to the kitchen to prepare tea, for a moment I thought of running out of the house in nervousness, but my promise to Sapra was the only reason holding me back. I then heard some rustling sound behind the closed door of an adjoining bedroom and realised that Tina was there inside, which reminded me of the task at hand, making me even more anxious. I tried to rehearse some of the mugged-up dialogues, but my mind seemed to turn completely blank. In a few minutes, Mrs Pal came with a cup of tea and sat on a chair opposite me.

While I was having tea, Mrs. Pal enquired about my wife and remembered the good time spent in the neighbourhood when both families lived in the same building. We also discussed some usual topics like weather, cantonment facilities, etc. As I finished tea, I looked at my watch. It was almost half an hour, and I had exhausted exchanging all the usual pleasantries.

"I hope Lieutenant Pal is not stuck with something very important in the office," I said. The statement was, in fact, a question.

"He had told me during lunch that he would be late in the evening, as there was something urgent, which he had to deal with today itself," Mrs Pal replied.

The time was running out. I could not continue waiting for Pal until late in the evening. Simultaneously, after spending more than half an hour at Pal's place, I could not contemplate returning without success, only to inform Sapra that Pal was not home. At that moment, I decided to speak out what I had rehearsed earlier in the day, even though my memory seemed to be failing me.

"Ma'am, I came here to discuss something important and personal with Lieutenant Pal but since he is not there, may I discuss it with you?" Hesitantly, I asked Mrs. Pal.

"Why not, if you feel that it can be discussed," she sounded a bit surprised.

My rehearsed dialogues vanished into thin air, as I heard myself say, "Ma'am, have you settled the marriage of Tina?" As I asked this question, I was surprised at the ease with which I could utter the sentence.

I was aware that it was quite possible that Tina in the adjoining room could overhear our discussion.

"No," Mrs Pal replied. She was evidently puzzled by my abrupt and unexpected question. "She is just a student and no one is in a hurry. But why do you ask this?"

This was the moment, I thought.

I hesitated for a while before saying, "I still feel that I should be discussing this matter with Lieutenant Pal. But since he is running late in his office, I will convey the proposal to you." I paused to take a deep breath.

"Lieutenant Rajeev Sapra is interested in Tina and wants to marry her. He wanted me to convey his proposal to Lieutenant Pal," I blurted out in a jiffy.

I could see that Mrs Pal was still a bit bewildered, trying to fathom what I was saying, but I continued. "If the proposal is acceptable to you, he would ask his parents to speak to your parents, but before that, he wants the consent of Tina." I looked at her face to gauge her reaction.

"The very purpose of my visit was to convey Sapra's proposal," I continued. "If you could ask Tina in confidence and Lieutenant Pal conveys her consent, Sapra would take the matter forward."

As I uttered these words, I realised that at least in the latter part of the conversation, my rehearsals helped me tremendously to say what was supposed to be conveyed.

While Mrs Pal was still allowing the proposal to sink in, I got up and said, "Now it is getting late and I must beg your leave, Ma'am. Lieutenant Sapra will eagerly wait for your response. And thanks for a nice cup of tea, good night," I said before quickly moving out of the main door.

ॐ ॐ ॐ

Six months seemed to have passed quickly after my wife left Ranchi to join her bank job at my native place. Immediately after our marriage in February 1982, Shashi decided to move with me to Ranchi for a few months by informing me that she had already got a 3-month leave without pay, though it was not initially planned. That's why I had made no prior request to get the family accommodation allotted to me before proceeding on annual leave for marriage.

So, I sent a telegram to the Adjutant of the unit informing him that on expiry of my leave, I would be reaching there along with my wife. I was not sure whether accommodation would be allotted to me at short notice of a few days and we were mentally prepared to stay in a one-room accommodation meant for bachelors in the officers' mess.

But on reaching Ranchi, we were pleasantly surprised when I was informed that a semi-furnished Type-IV house was already allotted to me. We were taken directly to the allotted accommodation from the railway station.

The accommodation was on the first floor of a double-storey building that had four 3-bedroom apartments. While two of the apartments were vacant, one of the flats on the ground floor, which was diagonally opposite our accommodation, was occupied by Pals.

Lieutenant A.K. Pal, an officer from the Brigade of Guards, was about three months senior to me. We found the Pals to be a good-natured couple. They were also newly married like us, and we made good acquaintances with them during our three-month stay there. When Pal and I were out on duty, both the ladies would spend some good time together.

Three months seemed to be over very soon. I then proceeded on a few days' casual leave to drop my wife at Bilaspur. After Shashi joined back at her job, I vacated the family accommodation and shifted back to the bachelors' quarters in the officers' mess. After about a month of my moving to the mess, quite an interesting incident took place.

Lieutenant AK Pal had a special guest at his house. The 'guest' took the bachelors of nearby Army units by storm, more particularly Lieutenant Rajeev Sapra, my battalion officer who was virtually blown over. The fancied guest was Lieutenant Pal's younger sister-in-law. About 18 years of age, Tina was a student of BA 2nd year, studying at Indore. She had come to visit her sister for a few days during her college vacations. Lieutenant Sapra noticed her during the farewell dinner of an outgoing Major General, General Officer Commanding (GOC) of the Mountain Division there.

The farewell dinner was organised in the mess of the Brigade of Guards. That evening, Tina was dressed in white baggy trousers and a smart, red-coloured top. With her fair complexion, she looked absolutely stunning in that outfit. Being fairly tall with a shapely figure, her charming presence was the centre of attraction for all the bachelor's at the party, and Sapra certainly was no exception.

About 24 years of age, Lieutenant Sapra himself was a handsome young man, blessed with an athletic build. Sapra's fair complexion with curly brown hair gave him the looks of a European. I remember when we both were undergoing the YOs' course at Infantry School Belgaum, many a time he was mistaken by many instructors and *ustads* to be a foreign trainee officer.

Sapra was three months senior to me, and both of us had joined the battalion almost at the same time. We were together for the YOs' course and shared a room for almost four months. We also had a memorable trip from Belgaum to Goa on bicycles, along with a few other friends.

Extremely fine and affable nature of Lieutenant Sapra was primarily responsible for a strong bond between the two of us. Most of the time, we were together in the battalion area, which, for some reason, did not go well with some of the seniors. Shockingly, an Adjutant of the battalion once passed a preposterous oral order that the two of us should never be seen together in the unit area!

Because of an interesting turn of events, I clearly remember the proceedings of that eventful Saturday evening in the guards officers' mess. As the party began, Lieutenant Sapra had his eyes following Tina while we were having a glass of beer each. A little while ago, he had confided in me that he had developed a strong liking for Tina.

After a while, during our beer session, he told me in confidence that he would like to marry Tina. I tried to persuade him to take some more time before arriving at such a vital decision in his life, but he was very firm and told me that it was love at first sight, at least for him. The only topic he wanted to discuss that evening was her beauty, grace, and charm. Several times, I tried to divert the discussion, but he would bring the conversation back to the same subject.

Farewell to a Major General-level officer is quite an important event for any officers' mess. Major Wilson, the 2IC of the guards battalion, was the master of the ceremony (MC) who initiated the proceedings of the evening by welcoming the guest of honour. He then made an announcement, which turned out to be a blessing in disguise for Sapra.

"Ladies and gentlemen," Major Wilson began. "Now, when the dinner is still a few hours away, we shall have some fun to make this evening a memorable one. In the next hour, we shall play the 'card couple' game," the Major continued.

"At the outset, I shall first invite the ladies to participate in the process. All the ladies present, including unmarried young ladies, are eligible to participate." Wilson eyed Tina as he uttered the above lines.

"Once we know the number of ladies participating, I will select an equal number of males out of the officers present, including bachelors, by a draw of lots. For the card game, I need the same number of male participants as that of ladies." Major Wilson seemed to have practised his lines very well.

I found Lieutenant Sapra unusually attentive to the announcement as Major Wilson continued, "As the next step, I shall proceed to make card couples. Suppose we have 20 female and male participants, I shall take out 20 cards from a pack of cards for female participants. From another pack of playing cards, I will then take out the same 20 cards for male participants."

The MC went on to explain the game, "Then I will request all the female participants to come forward. All the female participants will then pick up one card each from the female pack of 20 cards and keep that card with them. That's when I shall invite the chosen 20 male participants to come forward."

Wilson paused for a while before continuing, "The participating males will then be required to pick up one card each from another set of 20 cards meant for them. Finally, male and female participants having the same cards will become 'card couples' for this purpose."

There was a bit of murmur in the crowd as Major Wilson paused to take a breath. Lieutenant Sapra's attention was unflinching as Major Wilson continued, "All the card couples would then hit the dance floor and exhibit their dancing skills as a couple for the next one hour, with 2-3 short breaks in between. A jury led by Mrs Katoch, with two more lady wives not participating in the game, would be formed to select the best couple at the end of the dance session. The best cardcouple will win a surprise gift hamper!"

The announcement received a loud applause. Major Wilson then got busy inviting the participating ladies and writing down their names. Suddenly, I heard Lieutenant Sapra say in an inaudible whisper, "I would also participate if Tina does. In that case, I am certain that both of us shall make a couple for this game." I was surprised to see his wishful thinking and strong obsession with Tina.

Within minutes, the MC announced the names of 17 ladies who had opted to participate in the game. Sapra's prayers seemed to have been answered partially, as Tina's name was also there. Major Wilson then noted down the names of interested males and announced that 29 males had expressed their interest to play the game.

Needless to mention that Lieutenant Sapra had also got his name entered as one of the male aspirants to participate. Major Wilson then invited the outgoing Major General Katoch to select 17 male participants by way of drawing lots. 17 name slips were picked up by the general. Needless to say, Lieutenant Sapra's name-slip was also there.

All the participating ladies were then invited to draw one card each from the 'female' pack of 17 cards.

"In the meantime, let us charge our beer glasses," said Lieutenant Sapra. Both of us then moved to the bar and asked the barman to refill our glasses. Lieutenant Sapra had a few quick gulps and was ready for the game, fully confident that he was destined to partner with Tina.

After all the female participants had drawn their respective cards, Major Wilson invited the male participants one by one to pick up one card each from the pack of 17 cards meant for them.

16 male participants had been called. The last one obviously was Sapra. The MC then called out, "Who is the last male player? Please come forward and draw your card."

"It's me," Lieutenant Sapra called back loudly, half raising his right arm. With a stylish gait and a broad smile on his face, he walked up to the table, picked up the last card of the pack and came back.

Showing the card to me in confidence, he whispered, "It's the queen of hearts, Shekhar, and I am sure Tina is also holding the same card."

If he did not pair up with Tina, he was bound to be devastated, I thought.

"You can't be so sure. There is a very faint probability that she will also have a queen of hearts," I whispered back to him. By the look on his face, it was obvious that he did not like what I said. Dismissing my apprehension with a wave of his hand, he shifted his focus to the announcement from the stage.

"Hold your breath," announced the MC, "I am now going to announce the card couples for the dance game. I would now call the first lady participant and ask her to show her card to everyone. The male participant having the same card will then come forward, display his card, and the first couple will be formed. The same procedure will be repeated seventeen times to match all the participating ladies and gentlemen to form seventeen card couples before the game begins."

The MC Major Wilson then started the process. Lieutenant Rajeev Sapra seemed very anxious at the call of every name. Fifteen card couples had been formed and the names of neither

Tina nor Lieutenant Sapra figured in them, skyrocketing the expectations of Sapra.

"Number sixteen, Mrs Narayanan," was the next call. Mrs Narayanan walked up to the dais and handed over her card to Major Wilson. Our heartbeat quickened, and Sapra held my hand tightly. If the lady on the stage held any card other than the queen of hearts, pairing up of Sapra with Tina was a foregone conclusion.

While waiting for the next announcement, I could sense that Lieutenant Sapra had stopped breathing for the next few seconds. *Oh God, let it not be the queen of hearts.* With his eyes closed and the card in his hands, Sapra was praying.

Then we heard Major Wilson announce, "It is the seven of clubs."

Captain Mathur, who was holding a similar card, walked up to the stage to pair up with Mrs Narayanan. Lieutenant Sapra did not wait for the next announcement and literally shouted in excitement, "And I have the queen of hearts, the seventeenth card."

The seventeenth couple obviously was Lieutenant Sapra and Tina. It was a dream come true for Sapra. I congratulated him with a warm handshake. Excitedly, Sapra walked up to Tina, introduced himself and then both of them walked up to Major Wilson to hand over their respective cards.

All the card couples were then asked to wait on the dais for the next announcement. From a distance, I could see Lieutenant Sapra with a gleaming face, listening to Tina talking. He had suddenly become too conscious, and it was Tina who was keeping the conversation going. In the meanwhile, the ladies of the jury took their seats in front of the stage.

The beginning of the game was announced by the MC, and all the 'card couples' waited for the band to start playing. As the jazz band began to play a trendy tune, I took a lonely corner seat and kept observing my favourite couple. To me, both of them looked to be the most ideal couple out of the lot.

As I had known him, Lieutenant Sapra had never taken dancing seriously, but that day he was dancing superbly. Tina, on the other hand, turned out to be an excellent dancer and appeared to be the best among all the lady participants. Being the youngest couple, their energy level was pretty high, and the body chemistry between the two was splendid. They looked to be a divine couple.

Am I being biased?

There were a couple of breaks in between for the participants as well as for the band. During the breaks, Lieutenant Sapra would get a soft drink for Tina and gradually seemed to be more at ease in conversation with her. After an hour, the dance was over, and the jury became busy compiling the results.

Lieutenant Sapra led Tina towards the bar and offered her another soft drink while charging his own glass of beer. I walked up to them and congratulated Lieutenant Sapra for an outstanding performance. He then introduced me to Tina. I congratulated Tina for her stellar performance, and she gracefully thanked me.

"What are you doing tomorrow, Tina?" Lieutenant Sapra asked. Since the next day was a Sunday, I could guess what he was hinting at.

"Nothing special," she replied, smiling. "You know I am on holiday, and there is nothing specific I have in mind for tomorrow."

"Would you mind going out for a movie with me?" he asked her without an iota of hesitation. I had never thought that Sapra would move so fast. I was also pleasantly surprised at the ease with which he asked her for a movie date.

"Well..." Tina hesitated and thought over the proposal for a moment and said, "Well... you know, I am.... not really sure."

"Let me tell you that AK Pal is a close friend and batch-mate of mine. You may consult your *Didi* before confirming, if you so like," Sapra said without any hesitation. He seemed to have rehearsed his lines in his mind.

"Which movie is it?" she asked. She now appeared to be a bit reassured.

"Well, it is 'Farewell to Arms'. It is a good one and I am sure you will like it," he said, looking at her for a positive response.

"Okay, I'll come. And which show?" she said after thinking for a few seconds. As she agreed, a spark was visible in Sapra's eyes.

"It's the matinee, 3.00 pm. We'll also have lunch together in the city before the movie. I'll pick you up at around noon tomorrow. Is it okay?" he asked. I was pleasantly amazed at the ease with which he expanded the scope of the movie date.

"Are you also coming?" Tina looked at me and asked.

I was prepared for the question. "No," I said, "I am afraid I have some other engagement tomorrow."

"May I have your attention, ladies and gentlemen?" A loud announcement from Major Wilson interrupted our conversation. "Now that I have the decision of the jury with me, please hold your breath while I announce the winning couple of this gala evening."

There was a pin-drop silence. Sapra and Tina looked hopeful as the MC continued, "The best couple has been voted 3-0 by the jury, and the winners are Ms Tina and Lieutenant Rajeev Sapra! Give them a big hand."

Sapra was ecstatic, and Tina was all grins. Both of them shook hands and congratulated each other. I also congratulated both of them. Then there was a virtual commotion as most of the young officers came forward to greet both of them. A K Pal and his wife also came up and formally congratulated them.

"Ladies and gentlemen, please pay attention. One last ritual for this event is still left." Another loud announcement was made by the MC. "Now, I would request Mrs Katoch to please come over and present a surprise gift hamper to the winning couple."

Mrs Katoch, the wife of the outgoing GOC, gracefully walked up to the rostrum and handed over a big gift hamper to Sapra and Tina. All my battalion officers were keen to open the hamper, but Sapra decided to keep the surprise until the next morning.

After a few photographs by the cameraman, there was some free time for drinks and gossip. Tina excused herself and went to another corner with her sister and brother-in-law. For the remaining part of the evening, I had to listen to Sapra talking only about one obvious subject.

After the usual rituals of a farewell party like drinks, dinner, and farewell speeches, the party was finally over after midnight. While bidding her good night, Sapra reminded Tina about the next day's plan, which she acknowledged with a broad smile.

After we reached our mess, Sapra sat with me in my room and kept talking about Tina until 0330 hrs in the morning. He also thanked me several times for declining to accompany them to the movie with an excuse.

The next morning, we were woken up by our *Sahayak* with a cup of tea at around 1000 hrs. Sapra hurried to get ready and carefully selected his best dress for the day. After a quick bite at the breakfast table, he borrowed a scooter for conveyance from a senior officer, for which he had made a request the previous evening.

It was a few minutes to twelve when, with a lot of excitement, he waved at me and scooted away towards the house of Pals, which was just about a kilometre from the officer's mess.

It was around 1830 hrs that evening when Lieutenant Sapra returned. I had expected a bubbling and excited Sapra, keen to narrate the proceedings of the day to me in detail. But, to the contrary, he seemed rather dull and serious, if not annoyed.

On inquiring, he revealed that when he reached Pal's house to pick up Tina, Lieutenant and Mrs Pal were also dressed up to accompany them. Being a Sunday, both of them had also decided to entertain themselves with the movie. As per Lieutenant Sapra, the only part of the day that he enjoyed was while he was driving Tina to and from the city on the scooter and a few private moments while having *Dosas* for lunch at 'Sheetal Chhaya', a famous restaurant close to *Firayalal* crossing.

"I had hoped that I would get a seat next to her in the movie hall, but that did not happen," a dejected Sapra confided in me. "Tina sat in the corner seat, followed by Mrs Pal, Lieutenant Pal, and I found myself sitting next to Pal. This is not what I had expected," Sapra sounded utterly depressed.

During the next week, we remained busy with preparations for the visit of the new GOC to our unit, but the topic of discussion during the evenings did not change. Sapra kept yearning to see Tina but without success. Several times he told me that he was madly in love with her and desperately wanted to marry her.

During one of those evenings when Lieutenant Sapra was discussing Tina with me in the mess, Major Guleria walked in. He was posted as the Ground Liaison Officer (GLO) at the brigade HQ. Being a chronic bachelor, Major Guleria used to stay in a bachelor quarter in the mess with us. He had rejoined his duties only a day ago after availing his annual leave.

"Hi Sappy, I heard that you, along with a young female, were declared the best couple at the GOC's farewell dinner! By the way, who was your partner?" he asked. I could see Sapra blush and his fair complexion turn pink.

"It was Tina, sir, Lieutenant AK Pal's sister-in-law," Lieutenant Sapra replied. As Major Guleria showed interest in the discussion, Sapra narrated the whole incident of the farewell party and the movie date in detail to him.

"Are you seriously interested in her?" he asked after Sapra completed his narration.

Lieutenant Sapra suddenly turned very serious. After seeking permission from the Major to smoke, he took out a pack of cigarettes and lit one.

"I think I am, sir," he replied. "The more I think about it, the more I realise that I am madly in love with her. Yes, I want to marry her. But I doubt if I will be able to muster up the courage to propose to her."

"Don't you worry, Sappy, I will speak to Pals. I will call on them at their residence for breakfast tomorrow itself and put in a word for you in their minds. The rest is your luck," Major Guleria assured Sapra.

Since Guleria was also working in brigade HQ as a senior colleague of Pal, we were confident that he was capable of doing it for Sapra.

"Thank you, sir, I shall remain grateful to you." As Sapra spoke these words, I was sure that he had reached the point of no return. When we sat at the dinner table that evening, the details of the "Operation Proposal" were finalised between the three of us and by the time we finished our dinner, a definite action plan for Major Guleria was worked out.

That night, Lieutenant Sapra again kept discussing his hopes and apprehensions with me until late. Now the worry was, "Will she agree?" The fear of her refusal had begun to haunt him.

"She is a college student and she may already have a boyfriend," he wondered. "I am sure that she has the same feelings towards me, or maybe she doesn't," he brooded.

"Don't you worry, sir," I tried to explain. "You are smart, handsome, and above all, well-placed in life as an officer of the Indian Army. She has already been exposed to the Army way of life during the past two weeks, and I am sure she must have liked it." I tried to reassure him, "I am certain that her response will be in the affirmative."

Sapra seemed to agree with me when we finally slept. The next day morning, Major Guleria was not there for breakfast, and we knew for sure that he was having breakfast at the residence of Pals. Expecting to hear the good news from Guleria during lunch, both of us left for the office.

Five hours in the office seemed too long, as Lieutenant Sapra sat in my cabin after finishing his paperwork and kept pondering over the possible outcome of Major Guleria's discussion with Pals.

As we reached the mess for lunch at around 1330 hrs, with butterflies in his stomach, Sapra waited for Major Guleria. After about 15 minutes, we heard the rumble of the Royal Enfield motorcycle of Major Guleria and both of us came out to receive him. Lieutenant Sapra's anxiety hit the roof when the Major walked up to us after parking his bike.

He could sense that Sapra was stressed and gestured to us to come inside the mess. As the lunch was being laid, all three of us sat on a sofa. After a few moments of awkward silence, Major Guleria finally spoke in a low voice, "Mrs Pal had prepared a very elaborate breakfast, and it was delicious too."

Sapra obviously was not interested in knowing about the details of his breakfast. "But what about my message, sir? How did the discussion go?" asked an anxious Sapra.

What Major Guleria told him thereafter was an anti-climax. "Sorry, friend," said Major Guleria timidly, "I found it too difficult to handle. Though this was the very purpose of my going to the Pals, when the moment came, I realised that I did not have the knack for it."

Disbelief on Sapra's face was writ large, as Major Guleria continued, "Look, friend, I was not able to propose to anyone for myself during my heyday, and today I found it even more difficult to convey it on your behalf."

Crestfallen, Sapra was speechless for a while. I did not know how to console him, as we were back to square one. That evening, Lieutenant Sapra hardly spoke to anyone and had a few more drinks than usual. I was aware of his state of mind and left him alone for the evening. This was also the moment when I made the decision.

Sapra was a gem of a person. Although he was a couple of months senior to me in the highly hierarchical Army service, he never threw his weight around and always treated me as a good friend. So, I also decided to do something for him at the time when he was feeling low and hopeless.

The next morning, while having breakfast, I disclosed my intention to him. Though Sapra seemed delighted at my suggestion, he had some apprehensions as well.

"But Shekhar," asked Sapra, "will you be able to do it?"

"Why not, sir," I replied confidently. "I have decided that this evening I will go to their house and convey your feelings to Pal. Whether or not Tina agrees is your luck."

Considering a mixed reaction of hope and scepticism on his face, I thought of reassuring him further and said, "Look, sir, I was his immediate neighbour for about three months and am well acquainted with Mrs Pal as well. With that right, I can walk into their house without any hesitation."

"I agree," said Sapra, "and I know that you can easily go and visit them, but what I am concerned about is whether you would be able to say what you wish to."

The doubt in his mind was perhaps right. In our society, it is not the forte of a 25-year-old person to convey a matrimonial proposal on behalf of another young man of the same age, more so in the early 1980s.

During our spare time in the office that day, we planned a strategy to convey the message in the best possible words. He made me rehearse a few 'must-say' sentences. It continued during lunchtime, and we went over the final rehearsal again when the games time was about to end.

Dot at 1700 hrs, both of us left the games area on our bicycles. Pal's house was almost halfway to the brigade mess. Pedalling slowly and deliberately, he reminded me of a few crunch lines once again. "Don't worry, sir," I assured him, "God willing, it will be alright."

When Lieutenant Pals' house was just about 100 yards away, I could see that Sapra was more nervous than I was. As we reached in front of their house, I turned my bike to the right towards the compound of the building, and Lieutenant Sapra pedalled away straight towards the officers' mess after wishing me luck.

With a pounding heart, I got down from my cycle, pulled it onto its stand and went towards the entry door of Pals. After pressing the doorbell, I turned back to have a look at Sapra, but he had already disappeared in the far distance.

ও ও ও

Before Mrs Pal could say anything, I hurriedly came out of her house. I quickly rode my cycle towards the officers' mess, where I was sure that Sapra would be eagerly waiting. On entering the mess compound, I could see him standing outside his room and looking at me. With a broad smile on my face, I parked my cycle and went over to him.

Holding his hand, I pulled him inside his room and narrated the entire conversation. He was excited and sounded grateful to me. On my part, I was relieved that I could do what I had promised. Sapra was a bit relaxed now that the ball was in Tina's court. But the next question in our minds was - what would her response be?

I did not know whether Sapra slept that night. But when we met to go out for PT early morning the next day, he seemed quite tense. Cycling together towards the PT grounds, he expressed his misgivings about a possible delay or negative response from Pals.

After breakfast, we were about to proceed to the office when we saw Lieutenant Pal entering the main gate of the officers' mess compound on his scooter. With an expressionless face, he parked his scooter and walked up to us. I could see the anxiety gripping Sapra's face. I led Pal inside and offered him a seat on a sofa. We also sat next to him and waited to hear what he had to say.

"Rajeev," he said with a poker face, "I am damn annoyed with you." The tension mounted on Sapra's face as Pal continued. "Why did you send Shekhar to my house?" Sapra looked at me, apprehending the worst.

"You could have spoken to me yourself," Pal paused, and then suddenly flashed a broad grin on his face. He continued, "It would be my pleasure for life to be your co-brother. And when I say these words, I have the consent of Tina and her family to say so. The only catch is that she would complete her studies before we can plan the marriage."

Sapra was suddenly all smiles. He got up, embraced Pal and thanked him for a speedy and favourable response. He then turned to me and gave me also a tight hug. His eyes were wet with joy and other than uttering repeated thank-yous, he was at a loss for words. Later in the day, he went on to thank me several more times.

After a few weeks, I came to know that Sapra's parents had approached Tina's family and the engagement took place during Sapra's next earned leave. The marriage was solemnised in September 1984. Unfortunately, by then I was not present in the unit to welcome the lady.

A few years later, in the year 1987, I had a chance to meet the couple along with a few other officers and the lady wives when they visited Jwalamukhi Temple, a *Shaktipeeth* in Kangra District of Himachal, to erect a welcome gate there from the battalion funds to pay respects to the deity. I had a chance to host them all at my residence over lunch.

A few months before their visit, the Government had taken over the management of the temple by forming a trust and as Sub-Divisional Magistrate of Dehra, I was the ex-officio head of the Trust. Lest I forget to mention, the battle cry of the Dogra Regiment is "*Jwala Mata Ki Jai*". As part of the troop motivation effort, the officers and *Jawans* of various battalions of the Dogras visited the temple every now and then to pay their respects to the deity.

The incident finds itself in this book for a reason. There is always a life after the office hours. In the Army where it is not possible to socialise with the civilians, its own social life has to be fulfilling. The incident recounted by me provides a glimpse into a small part of the Army social life in peace stations, including the life of the young officers.

This anecdote also unfolds a strong bond among the service officers, created by a unique sense of regimentation. In the absence of a strong feeling of regimentation, it will be difficult for any battalion or regiment to go to war and fight for the country.

Chapter-IV

A Raid Across the Border

"Soldiers generally win battles; generals get credit for them"

–Napoleon Bonaparte

A small detachment of my men, responsible for providing the covering fire to the group I was leading, had taken up the position on a raised platform with a Light Machine Gun (LMG). Close to the Line of Control (LoC), the task assigned to the detachment was to provide us with effective fire cover from any possible enemy interference from its nearest post or by any hostile patrol passing by.

Our discrete movements helped us to quietly cross the LoC through the enemy minefield gaps in the cover of darkness. After crossing over to the enemy territory, I stopped crawling for a while to appreciate the ground situation. The nearest enemy post was about 800 metres to our half-left in the northwest direction. There was no movement of any kind around us. Satisfied with the progress, I signalled the boys behind me to follow my crawl.

It was well past midnight. The faint moonlight was not bright enough to give us away to the enemy. After a noiseless crawl for another fifteen minutes or so, on getting a soft nudge on my ankle from Havaldar Sohan Lal, I stopped again. Responsible for navigation, Sohan Lal was right behind me. In a hushed whisper, he told me that the bearing of the compass and grid reference on the map suggested that we were very close to our objective. He then indicated towards a hill slope, which was about 50 metres ahead of us.

I could see a shallow concave-shaped cavity formed by a massive rock overhanging on a slope. The entire area around the cave was devoid of any vegetation. The shallow cavity on the slope seemed to be an ideal place for camping at night. I looked around for any sentry guarding the area, but there was none. Zunaid and his men perhaps felt safe sleeping inside the cave unguarded, being on the other side of the LoC.

To be certain, I signalled to two of my boys to go crawling from the left flank and the other two from the right of the hideout to see again if any sentry was protecting the cave. In that case, we had to silence him first to maintain the element of surprise. In about fifteen minutes, all four boys came back and signalled that there was none.

The next move was to get closer to the objective. All of us quietly began crawling and moved further up. As we drew nearer, I could see a few sleeping bags inside the shallow cave. Yes, Zunaid Khan and his men were sleeping in olive green sleeping bags. We silently entered the open cavity and immediately seized five automatic rifles lying by the side of a sleeping bag.

With a loaded Sten gun, I nudged one of the sleeping bags hard. The man inside moved and mumbled something. Simultaneously, my other companions also poked their guns hard against the other four men sleeping. Soon, all of them were awake and began struggling to wriggle out of their sleeping bags.

"Don't move, we are the Indian Army," I said with a forced whisper, making sure that I was not audible to the enemy post close by. "Put your hands behind your heads and kneel."

A sudden interruption in their sleep had left Zunaid and his men bewildered. Several soldiers pointing their weapons at their heads further compounded their confusion. It was obvious that they didn't expect the Indian Army to capture them on the other side of the LoC.

≈ ≈ ≈

Earlier, in the afternoon of the previous day, I had received a call from the Commanding Officer (CO) over the field telephone. He informed me that as per the inputs received from the intelligence agencies, a wanted Kashmiri separatist named Zunaid Khan was camping inside enemy territory close to our location.

As per the information, Zunaid, who was a close associate of Maqbool Butt (also known as the first Kashmiri separatist), was camping in a hideout on the other side of the border with his 4-5 men. It was apprehended that Zunaid Khan was intending to cross over to the Indian Territory on the following day with the help of the adversary Army.

Zunaid was part of a Kashmiri separatist outfit called Jammu Kashmir Liberation Front (JKLF) and was wanted in many criminal cases in the state of J&K. Later, in the year 1984, the top leader of the JKLF, Maqbool Butt, was hanged for various killings, but the fate of his associate Zunaid Khan is not known.

Detailed information was given in a coded wireless message, which included the grid reference of the camping location. The task was crisp and clear - to raid the hideout camp that night and capture the separatist and his associates, alive or dead.

There was hardly any time for detailed planning. The grid reference, when plotted on the map, indicated that his hideout was located about six kilometres northwest from the Ashok post and about a kilometre inside the other side of the LoC.

After estimating that the total time required for the operation would be five to six hours, I selected ten spirited soldiers from all four posts along with a young Junior Commissioned Officer (JCO) named Naib Subedar Ram Chand. Another team of five soldiers under Havaldar Khub Chand, with a Light Machine Gun and their firearms, was also to accompany us to take a position near the LoC during the raid to cover our movement across the border.

It was only a couple of weeks ago that the Commanding Officer had appointed me as the officiating Company Commander of Alpha Company, which was deployed on the forward posts. Previously, the company commander had to leave for Extra-Regimental Employment (ERE).

The next morning, I climbed up to the forward posts with five soldiers, two mules, and a couple of porters carrying heavy baggage and other provisions. It took more than five hours of stiff climbing to reach the Ashok post, located at an altitude of about 11,800 feet above MSL. The HQ of the Alpha Company was located at Ashok, which became my location for the next few months.

Alpha Company was responsible for guarding the border in that area and was deployed to protect the border with four forward posts, i.e. Ashok, Piku, Riku, and Anthony. While the Riku and Anthony posts were to the right flank of Ashok, the Piku Post was to its left. All four posts were on four hill peaks, all about one kilometre apart, on a single longish mountain feature facing the enemy positions in the north.

The border in that area was not guarded by a linear defence line, and only the higher features on the LoC were occupied by the Indian troops. The gaps were covered by anti-personnel mines and continuous patrolling. While strict vigil was kept during the day to stop any movement from across the border, during the night, every post sent out mobile patrols to keep the gaps effectively covered and make sure that no unauthorised person crossed over.

Almost at a similar altitude across the border, about five hundred metres north of our location, there were three posts of the enemy on three hillocks. The enemy positions were manned by a section (ten soldiers) each. The Army on the other side also followed the tactics of covering the gaps between the posts with mines and patrolling.

The overall in charge of all three posts of the adversaries was a JCO. An officer of the rank of Captain would visit their posts only once a month from HQ for a couple of hours, only to return the same evening. The Indian Army, on the other hand, is always led by its officers from the front even at high-altitude locations, howsoever tough the weather conditions may be. This, by itself, made a lot of difference in the motivation levels of troops on the two sides.

Between the Ashok and the Piku Posts, there was a pass, and anyone coming from the other side of the border had to cross it. A mule track was left uncovered by minefields for human movement through the pass during the daytime. The remaining gaps were covered by randomly placed anti-personnel mines.

By and large, this part of the border was generally peaceful. During the entire tenure of our unit in the area, we never experienced any incident of cross-border firing.

As an officer in charge of the company, I was supposed to keep close coordination between all four posts, which were commanded by one JCO each. Radio silence was maintained throughout, except at the designated time for a couple of minute slots (which were changed daily) when the wireless sets were switched on to communicate the daily security update to the CO in coded language.

There were regimental field telephone lines providing a safer alternative for intra-company communication and for communicating with the battalion HQs. This mode of communication, however, was not reliable, as due to heavy snow and the occasional boulders rolling down the slopes, the telephone lines would snap every now and then.

To plan and execute the mini-operation to capture Zunaid Khan, I had to rely on the enemy's minefield layout map of the area supplied to us by our intelligence agencies. I identified a crossing place through a few gaps in the minefields in the enemy area. A few gaps are generally left in front of the defences to facilitate the movement of the incoming and outgoing patrols. The chosen gap, however, was very close to one of the enemy posts.

I was aware that due to limited manpower of the adversary troops, their night patrolling was virtually negligible. Since there was still a possibility of encountering an enemy patrol while crossing the border, the covering fire had to be planned to take care of any such contingency.

Just like most Army operations, the key to the success of this low-key operation was to maintain surprise until the last minute and to ensure not to alert either the hideout camp or the nearest enemy post. If we were not able to maintain surprise, the whole operation would either fail or entail several casualties. And both the above outcomes were not acceptable. Avoiding running into any enemy patrol was equally important.

We carried out a few dry rehearsals during the day as per planning. After some rest in the evening, we left our location at around 2200 hrs. The route to the objective involved going down a gradual slope. We walked for an hour and a half before crossing over the LoC through the identified gaps.

All the separatists hurriedly knelt and bent forward with their hands behind their heads. My men searched them for any small arms on their person. Naib Subedar Ram Chand recovered a pistol in a holster from one of the captives, suspected to be Zunaid Khan. The description of his appearance received from the intelligence agencies and the recovery of the pistol reconfirmed his identity to us.

My boys tied the hands of all the captives tightly with a rope, taped their mouths, and then tied them all together in a row with a common rope. They were ordered to move with us without making any unnecessary sounds. I warned them that if any of them made any noise or did any mischief, all of them would be shot in the head.

Since the separatists were in our custody, we decided to walk across the LoC to quickly move out of the enemy territory. The covering fire team also joined us after we crossed over to the Indian side and began our return journey. Five of my *Jawans* kept their guns shoved against their backs as we walked towards Ashok post, following the same route.

The operation was a complete success, as we could apprehend the separatists alive without firing a single round. Without any casualties on any side, we could get a rich haul of weapons and ammunition from them. On the radio set with us, I transmitted a coded success signal to Ashok, which the company JCO was expected to re-transmit onwards to the HQ immediately.

During our movement away from the LoC towards our pickets, Zunaid Khan asked me why he was being arrested. I did not reply to him and kept asking all of them to keep moving fast. A gradual climb to Ashok took us around 3 hours to return.

It was around 0500 hrs in the morning when we reached the Ashok post. Subedar Dharam Chand informed me that the CO wanted me to call him over the field telephone immediately. When I called him, the CO congratulated me on accomplishing the mission. He also informed me that Lieutenant Surender, along with a few *Jawans,* had already left the battalion HQ to bring the captives to the unit HQ.

I kept all five prisoners tied and locked in three separate bunkers, with armed guards outside. I had a few cookies and a hot cup of tea before taking a short nap. In another five hours, Lieutenant Surender with his team reached the Ashok post. After a little rest and an early lunch, Surender and his men headed back to the HQ along with the captives.

After a few days of this incident, I received a bunch of newspapers for the previous few days and one of the newspapers carried a small front-page box news with the caption, **"Zunaid Khan Arrested"**. The news item read as follows:

"Zunaid Khan, a close associate of Maqbool Butt and the co-founder of the Jammu Kashmir Liberation Front, along with four of his associates, was nabbed last night near the LoC when he tried to sneak into Indian Territory. Several automatic weapons were also seized from them. Zunaid Khan is wanted by the police of five Indian states in several criminal cases pending against him.

After receiving a tip-off from the intelligence agencies, in a swift operation, the Indian Military Forces apprehended Zunaid Khan and his men from a hideout in North Kashmir near the LoC."

No further details were provided.

Chapter-V

The Enemy?

"A leader is one who knows the way, goes the way and shows the way"

–John Cavin Maxwell

Yet Another Raid

A few days after the raid to apprehend Zunaid Khan was carried out, yet another raid was conducted. One early afternoon, the JCO in charge at the Riku post, Naib Subedar Rup Chand, spoke to me over the field telephone and asked permission to come to me, as he wanted to discuss something in person. I called him over to the Ashok post in the afternoon that day. He wanted a decision from me and narrated an incident to me.

He said, "Yesterday two persons from village Ranzalwan came to me and complained against a *Dera* (refers to a group in colloquial, generally one family) of *Gujjars*. They informed that the *Dera* members were carrying a few weapons and were involved in stealing the goats & cattle of the villagers, unauthorisedly crossing over to the other side of the border to sell the stolen cattle and in all probability, acting as informers of the Pak Army as well," Rup Chand continued.

"When I checked the records, the *Dera* was not registered with us or any of our four posts. That meant that they had not shown their passes or gun licences to us before entering the restricted border area. Since the *Dera* was based closer to the Riku post, I, along with three Jawans, went to check their passes and asked them why they had failed to register with us." Rup Chand seemed a bit anxious as he recounted the details.

"In all, they are 15 in number, including 5 adult males, 6 females and the remaining 4 minor children. The *Dera* has about forty cattle and a few goats & sheep." Naib Subedar Rup Chand was now charged up, it seemed.

"Their attitude was highly arrogant, and they mentioned that they need not show the passes to anyone. Abdul Karim, the *Dera* head, also asserted that anyone wanting to check the passes should have come over to them. I could see a double-barrel gun with one of the persons named Mushtaq. When I asked both Abdul and Mushtaq to come with me to the post for registration and verification of passes and gun licences, they flatly refused." He paused to take a breath before continuing.

"Without the use of any force, I could somehow convince them to come with us. As they started moving up with us, all the 6 women of the *Dera* also started following us," Rup Chand went on.

"We had hardly come about 100 metres uphill when Abdul Karim jumped backwards and started rolling down the gradual slope. I followed him with my men and caught hold of him again after a few minutes. But the women of the *Dera*, who were following us, encircled us all and pleaded with me to leave their men alone." The Naib Subedar continued with the details.

"At that stage, one of the women, perhaps the wife of Abdul, started using derogatory words against the Indian Army, calling us all a 'band of goons 'and all the officers as '*awaras*'. She accused that Army personnel were interested either in the females of *Deras* or in their goats and sheep. She further mentioned that they had good links in civil administration and one of her cousins was a Minister in J & K Government. A strong feeling of contempt in the eyes of Rup Chand was more than visible as he recollected the incident.

"Another woman, a teenage sister of Karim, went to the extent of saying that if we took their men along, she would also come along, and tell the nearby villagers and the civil police that we took her to our post forcibly and tried to rape her," Rup Chand said with mixed expressions of anguish and disdain on his face.

"By then, Abdul Karim also got encouraged and sarcastically told me that in case I was so interested in their females, he would get his sister married to me, because as per him, I had an eye on her. *Sa'ab,* for a married person like me having a family, it was not only embarrassing but insulting as well." By the tone of his spoken words, the JCO sounded to be deeply hurt by the false allegations levelled by the tribal group.

"At that point in time, my *Jawans* started losing patience and pestered me to allow them to use force, but in the absence of your approval to do so, I refused. I decided to come back to the post and bring the issue to your notice." As he continued, the incident as narrated by Rup Chand seemed to be devoid of any exaggeration.

"Sir, the allegation of crossing the border against them is quite serious and needs to be investigated. The validity of their border area passes and gun license also needs to be verified. But before proceeding with this matter, your orders are required. If you approve, Sa'ab, I would go to them again with more manpower and drag the buggers forcibly to the post." As he finished with the complete account of the incident, Rup Chand looked at me, hoping for my instant approval.

After listening to Naib Subedar Rup Chand, I pondered over the situation for a while. In that area, any civilian coming closer to the LoC needed a pass from the local administration or the police authorities. Such civilians were then required to register themselves with the nearest Army post before taking their cattle closer to the LoC for grazing. Any firearm carried by them was also supposed to be declared and logged in along with its licence.

The *Dera* had obviously violated the above rules. But more serious was the allegation of espionage and crisscrossing the international border, which required to be thoroughly investigated. But then, if I allowed free use of force to apprehend them, it had its own hazards. While doing so, the weapons could be fired from either side, which could snowball into a big issue. Any false allegation by the women could add to our woes by creating a serious controversy.

Suddenly, I became clear in my mind about the course of action. There was no point in acting in isolation. I asked the telephone operator to put me through to the CO. Colonel Mehra was on casual leave, and Major DS Behuria was officiating.

After Major Behuria came on the line, I explained the entire incident to him. He immediately gave his decision, saying, "You go yourself with full force and raid the *Dera* in a day or so and bring the bloody culprits to your post for investigations. Then send me a written report through a special messenger."

I was aware that asking for written orders in such matters would be expecting too much and the operation had to be planned with due care, in a manner that least force was used and the situation did not go out of hand. Any operation involving the local and civilian population, if not handled with care, could snowball into a serious trouble later.

I started the preparations and selected 15 spirited soldiers to conduct the raid in the wee hours of the night after the next. The following morning and the entire day, we carried out a few rehearsals, after which I gave a detailed briefing to the raiding party.

On the designated night, we set off for the Riku post at around midnight, as the location of the *Dera* was more easily accessible from there. Before heading towards the *Dera* location from Riku, I reiterated the verbal orders for the raid to the entire team. It was made clear to everyone that no unnecessary sounds would be made.

We left the Riku post at around 0230 hrs. It involved around 40 minutes of walking on a gradual downward slope. While moving, my mind was occupied; what if trouble broke out during the raid and we were forced to use weapons, resulting in casualties?

I must make sure that no weapons are used.

After walking down the gradual slopes, we found ourselves on a steep slope over a narrow and dangerous path. The area was bereft of any trees, with only ankle-high grass all around. The night being dark, we were required to use battery-operated torches while going down the uneven steps over the cliff. Towards the end of the slope, we had to cross a *nala* filled with muck from a melting glacier, which was slippery to walk on.

The descent was over in another 20 minutes when we reached a flat and barren piece of land, almost half the size of a hockey ground. Towards the other end of the ground, there was a sudden drop of the hill, with a thick coniferous forest. Naib Subedar Rup Chand quietly pointed towards the corner of the ground, closer to the forest, where three tented huts could be seen 10 metres apart from each other.

So, the Dera is camping here!

We split into three groups and moved closer to the tents to encircle them. In the absolute calm of early morning, only our soft footsteps made a faint sound. Then all of a sudden, there was some movement inside one of the huts encircled by Naib Subedar Rup Chand's party, while the other two tents seemed still. A middle-aged woman popped her head outside through a flap of the tent. After giving a puzzled and scared look, she immediately pulled her head inside the tent. I signalled to Rup Chand to open the flaps of the tent.

Naib Subedar followed my instructions and lifted one of the front flaps of the tent but hurriedly dropped it and stepped aside with a confused look on his face. Alarmed, I asked him in a forced whisper, "What happened?"

"Sir..r..sir..," He stammered, "All the women inside are n..na...nak…. not wearing any c..clo..clothes"

We allowed the ladies a few minutes to dress up. Later, I was told by one of the local porters that Gujjars in that area generally slept without any clothes on. While we were waiting to get the women out of their tent, surprisingly, there was still no movement in the other two tents.

Are the others still sleeping?

In the meantime, I asked one of the boys to enter the second tent. He peeped inside and reported that the tent was vacant. I lifted a flap and found 4-5 unkept beddings on the ground, indicating that the occupants had hurriedly fled.

There were four children in the third tent, all between 7 and 14 years of age, who had just woken up. It was strange to find a *Dera* camping without a male member, that too at night. *So, they managed to slip away.*

In another direction, there were some cows, goats, and sheep in a temporary enclosure. Surprisingly, there was no dog to guard the herd, which was unusual.

I then turned to the first bivouac. By then, six women were coming out and Naib Subedar Rup Chand asked all of them to line up. At that very moment, the children also came out of their tent and joined the women.

"Where are Abdul Karim, Mushtaq, and the others?" I asked them loudly.

Seeing a number of Army personnel with their weapons pointed at them, all the children and women seemed terrified. One of the women then replied, "Sa'ab, all the men have gone to Dandipura and will come back tomorrow."

I knew for sure that it was a blatant lie. After an altercation with my men a couple of days ago, they were perhaps on guard and could see the occasional lighting of torches on the cliff while we walked down. In all probability, they hurriedly slipped into the thick forest below or crossed over to the other side of the unmanned portion of the LoC close by.

Another possibility was that their dogs alerted them and they slipped out. This belief was further strengthened by the fact that there was not even a single dog near the *Dera*. The dogs perhaps followed their fleeing masters into the forest. Looking for the culprits in thick vegetation would be like searching for a needle in a haystack. If they had crossed over, then in any case they were out of our reach, at least temporarily. *Have we failed in our mission?*

Naib Subedar Rup Chand suggested that we take the children with us to our posts. He was certain that such an action would force the missing males of the *Dera* to report to us themselves. Havaldar Shri Ram's advice was that it would be more effective if we took the women also along. Another suggestion was that we could take some of their goats along and the absconders would be arm-twisted to present themselves on their own.

The women and the children were carefully listening to our conversation. Suddenly, one of the ladies pleaded, 'Sa'ab, please take two or three goats for mutton and leave us alone.'

I ignored her offer as my mind was busy thinking. I quickly considered all the suggestions of my team. To me, involving the children in the whole affair was out of the question.

The suggestion of taking all or a couple of women along was fraught with several inherent and added complications. If I did that, the possibility of false allegations of misbehaviour by the women was always there. It was unethical too. *No, not this alternative.*

The third option to take a few goats along appeared to be even more absurd to me. Firstly, the men in uniform were not supposed to take goats and cattle along. Furthermore, we could be accused of stealing the goats from the *Dera* and the number of goats could be exaggerated to file a false police complaint for theft, putting us on the defensive.

A different line of action was already lurking in my mind. I was positive that my idea would work. It was already around 0500 hrs in the morning. All six women and four children were made to sit in front of the tents, facing us. Their arrogance, which I had heard about from Rup Chand, was nowhere visible. They were rather subdued and submissive, perhaps overawed by the display of force and intent by us.

I went closer to them and sat down in front of them. After waiting for a moment, I said, "Listen, our aim of coming here was to take Abdul Karim and Mushtaq along, as they have not complied with regulations and there are some serious allegations against them which require investigation."

All of them listened to me attentively, as I continued, "We are not the foes and our aim is not to harass anyone. Any inconvenience caused to you all is only because of your attempts to wrongfully shield your men. With the non-compliance of the Government regulations and misbehaving with my men, they have challenged the Government."

I waited for a moment, looked at their faces and continued, "You may also be aware that the Army has been entrusted with enormous responsibility and authority in these forward areas. We can arrest you all and take you to our post as captives until your men show up. But I shall not do that because I do not want to harass you for something that you have not done." I paused again for a while to take a deep breath.

Naib Subedar Rup Chand was looking at me with dismay. Utter disapproval of what I had mentioned was writ large on his face. The *Dera* women were, however, listening to me attentively, curious to know what I wanted to say next.

"I know that the culprits are hiding somewhere nearby," I went on, "But there is no point in continuing with this game of hide and seek. Since we have the orders to get hold of them, we shall get them, no matter how many times we may have to come. Next time there will be more men and more weapons with us to ensure that Karim and Mushtaq are not able to slip away. So, it is in the interest of all of you to advise your men to report to us on their own at the earliest so that undue harassment to you and your children is avoided."

I got up and looked at my men and asked them to get back.

"Is that all Sa'ab?" asked one of the women. "Don't you want some goats from us?"

"No," I replied sternly, "We get more than enough rations and mutton from the Government. We do not need anything from anyone."

For a little while, the women spoke to each other in their own language, which was difficult to comprehend. Finally, the eldest of them said, "please forgive us, Sa'ab. We misunderstood you. We had harboured negative views about the Army, mainly fuelled by hearsay. A couple of times earlier, whenever we ran into an Army patrol or a picket, we escaped by offering a goat or two." The woman glanced at the faces of my team before continuing.

"We had heard some fabricated stories about the molestation of local women by the Army men. This year when we came here, we were determined not to cooperate with the Army, which was the reason for our misbehaviour. But we can assure you, Sa'ab, whenever our men come back, we will ask them to report to your post." I could see truthfulness in her eyes as the lady spoke.

"I will wait only for a day," I said firmly, "after which I shall have no option but to use brute force." I turned back and ordered my men to get organised for returning.

15 minutes after we started to move up the hill, the early morning sun greeted us. Down below on the flat piece of land, all the *Dera* women and children could be seen standing outside their tents and occasionally waving their hands at us.

"They have fooled us, Sa'ab," I heard my JCO say. "These women are very clever and know how to handle a situation like this. Soon, we may have to raid their *Dera* again from a different direction."

Naib Subedar Rup Chand had served in the Army for about 20 years, and whatever he spoke reflected the wisdom of his experience. However, as the team leader, I had decided on what seemed to be the best alternative in the given circumstances.

"Instead of jumping to conclusions, let's wait for a day," I said. "I am sure these guys will come to us on their own."

As I uttered these words, I could hear a muffled snigger from Rup Chand walking behind me, which I ignored.

As we moved further up, I asked the radio operator to convey the outcome of the raid to the HQ, which he did. A little while later, there was a message on the wireless that Major Behuria wanted to speak to me.

I immediately connected with him on his personal wireless set.

"So, your operation was abortive, I believe?" I heard him say.

"Not really abortive, sir," I replied curtly, "I am certain to get the culprits at our post within the next 24 hours."

I could sense that the 2IC was not convinced, as he said, 'Give me a detailed account of the operation over the field telephone after you reach Ashok. Over and out'.

After my radio conversation with Major Behuria, we walked quietly for a few minutes. Breaking the awkward silence, Naib Subedar Rup Chand asked me, "Sir, do you really believe that these chaps are going to come to us on their own?"

I did not reply. Yes, there was a chance that they might not turn up. In that case, the next course could be initiated only after waiting for a day. Uneasy silence prevailed on the remaining route. As we reached the Riku post, a few boys and Naib Subedar Rup Chand dropped out there. After having a cup of hot tea there, I, along with the rest of the soldiers, walked back to Ashok.

On the same evening at around 1700 hrs, I received a call from Naib Subedar Rup Chand, informing me that Karim and Mushtaq had reported at his post. They kept reporting for the next one week to be part of the investigations. After a detailed inquiry into all the allegations against them, they were found guilty of only one offence – not reporting their arrival to the nearest Army post along with the permit and not registering their gun licence there.

The charge of crossing the LoC was not proven, and their gun was found to have a valid licence. Theft of sheep and cattle by the *Dera* members was a matter to be looked into by the civil administration, and the complainants were asked to approach the local police. Considering the nature of violations, they were let off with a stern warning not to repeat the misconduct in the future.

Life at the Posts

The remoteness of the forward posts was more like solitude. There was hardly any link with the latest happenings around the world, as the newspapers would reach in a bunch after several days. The only way to keep abreast of the outside world was to listen to the radio news, the short-wave reception of which would be clearer only after the fall of night.

At night, when the radio reception would improve, one could tune into many foreign stations, and one of the best sources of news would be the BBC. All India Radio, Srinagar, and the Doordarshan News were the sources of the national news. The complete detailed national and world news would, however, be available only when the old newspapers were received after a few days.

There were no villages in the near vicinity. For obvious reasons, one could not mix with the troops beyond a limit, but I did play Tennikoit ring (also called Tennis ring) with my soldiers at a flattish area near the Ashok post in the afternoons. I had never played ring earlier and never considered it a game worth any physical activity. But when I played it there, I discovered that just like any other sport, it was quite entertaining, absorbing and a bit tiring as well. It seemed to be a perfect sporting activity at that higher altitude location, having insufficient oxygen.

Though we had a volleyball with us, I knew that one strong smash would send the ball rolling down into the hostile territory on the other side. We could never think of playing badminton due to the strong breeze blowing most of the time.

I had a lot of spare time there, particularly after sunset when my job required me either to remain awake until at least midnight or to get up after midnight almost daily. As the officer in charge of the company, it was mandatory for me to carry out one or two surprise checks on the night guards and patrols. Proximity to the enemy required all of us to remain vigilant all the time.

There was hardly any paperwork at the posts. The only task was to guard the borders of the country. In the absence of any hostilities from the other side of the border, I generally had a lot of spare time during the day. I utilised this time to brush up on my general knowledge as well as two academic subjects that I had planned to offer as optional subjects for the civil services examination.

Some nomadic groups of local tribes of Jammu & Kashmir, namely Bakarwals and Gujjars, would generally move in that area along with herds of their cattle from one place to the other throughout the year. During late summers, they would climb up the mountains with their sheep and cattle. Green and nutritious grass in the higher grasslands is considered very nourishing for the cattle, for which they were granted grazing rights by the State Government. After the onset of autumn, they would take their cattle back to the lower altitudes before the snowfall commenced.

An Amazing Incident

It happened during the middle of August when a small group from a *Bakkarwal* tribe crossed the pass closer to the Piku Post on the Indian side and halted below the post for a little longer than usual. Observing through my binoculars, I called up the JCO in charge of Piku Post over the field telephone and asked him to send a small armed patrol to find out why it was taking them so long.

Four *Jawans* with their weapons were sent there, who spoke to them for a while before returning. After about an hour, the tribal group moved on. Almost at the same time, the patrol also reached the Ashok post to report to me.

Naik Baldev, the patrol in charge, informed me that one of the women in the tribal group was in the advanced stage of pregnancy and upon reaching that location, she started having labour pains, forcing the group to halt there for a while. Baldev also informed me that upon his arrival, he was told that the lady had just delivered a baby.

For me, it was extremely difficult to visualise a pregnant woman delivering a child in the biting cold at that altitude. I was further told that after about half an hour of the delivery, the tribal group moved ahead by making the new mother sit on a mule's back with the newborn baby wrapped in a woollen shawl across her body.

The narration of the incident by Baldev left me wondering. Riding on the mule back in hilly terrain during the advanced stage of pregnancy was something one could hardly perceive as feasible in the towns and cities. More than that, giving birth to a baby in the open and biting cold at that altitude without supervision by any healthcare expert seemed bizarre to me. For a new mother to ride on the mule back with a newborn within half an hour of childbirth was also unimaginable.

Foes?

Earlier, at the end of July, there were continuous rains for about three days, and the temperature dipped considerably. Generally, the monsoons do not penetrate that far in the north. The unusually prolonged spell of rain was perhaps caused by western and local disturbances.

While it was still raining, on the third day, one of the *Jawans* from the observation post came running to me and reported that three soldiers from the other side of the LoC were coming towards our post. I came out of my bunker with my weapon and observed the area through the binoculars. A JCO from the other side, holding a white flag in his hand, accompanied by two soldiers, was approaching our defences. All three of them were unarmed. The JCO began to wave the white flag sideways as he came closer to the LoC.

I asked Subedar Dharam Singh to go closer with a few boys and asked a section of my post to cover their movement. The rain had turned into a light drizzle by then. Subedar Dharam Singh, along with four more armed soldiers, went as close as 15 metres to the LoC and asked them what the matter was.

The conversation was not audible to me due to the howling of the strong breeze. After a few minutes, Subedar Dharam Singh came back to brief me. Due to continuous rain during the previous days, the firewood of the troops on the other side of the LoC had got completely drenched, and they were not able to ignite it. Dharam Singh said that the JCO was requesting for one jerrican of kerosene to ignite their wet firewood to make a fire in the *bukharis* to keep warm.

I was aware that the Pakistani Army personnel were given only fuel wood to burn in *bukharis*, as their country could ill afford to supply the kerosene oil to its troops even at the high-altitude posts where the troops had to brave extremely cold weather. On our side, the Indian Army used to supply sufficient kerosene, enabling us to use the *bukharis* as and when the weather warranted.

I considered the request for a while. My first thought was to say a blunt no, but the conduct of the troops on the other side had been quite friendly during the recent past. We had no personal animosity with the troops deployed on the other side. Moreover, the two countries were also not at war. Considering the situation from a broader humanitarian perspective, I asked the company JCO to give them kerosene as well as a few bottles of rum.

After a while, a jerrican of kerosene along with some rum was handed over by my men to the soldiers waiting at the LoC. They waved at us and went back to their post.

The other side was so obliged that the entire manpower of ten personnel came out in the open and shouted "*Shukriya Hindostan*" slogans for several minutes. I was later told by the company *Jawans* that after that incident, the relations between the two sides improved further and both sides would wish each other on festivals like *Eid* and *Diwali*.

A few months spent at the forward posts gave me a detailed insight into the life of a soldier in the operational area. Leading the men under extreme weather conditions requires excellent man-management skills, and the lessons learned there remain instilled in my behaviour, which helped me immensely in some crunch situations later in my career.

The Indian Army offers a career with plenty of built-in adventure. If the formidable conditions are taken as training and adventure, one can learn a lot, which I did. After having worked in civil services and the corporate world later in my career, I realised that no other career offers an experience which is as rich, absorbing and unique as that in the Army.

Chapter-VI

Selection to the Army

"For our tomorrow, they gave their today."

–A famous quote about the soldiers

"Shekhar, I have forwarded your application, along with mine, for the Combined Defence Services (CDS) Exam to the UPSC," Ashu said smiling, which compounded my confusion.

"Here is your balance amount I am returning to you, after keeping the cost of the Application Form, the registered letter and the fees," he said, returning some change to me.

"But I never applied! You know that I am pursuing my MBA and have no plans to join the Army!" I strongly objected.

It was in April 1978. After completing the Master's in Economics in 1977, I was pursuing an MBA at Himachal Pradesh university, Shimla. Those were the days when many of the much-fancied business schools of today did not exist, and the MBA was offered only at a few Indian universities with a very small number of seats.

The reason was obvious. With a limited growth of the corporate sector by then, the career opportunities were also few. The first preference of most of the management graduates was the public sector. In other words, even in the corporate world, the students preferred the jobs in the public sector undertakings.

This anecdote about my joining the Indian Army as a commissioned officer is quite interesting. The turn of events convinced me early in life that in addition to a major role played by hard work, destiny also has an equally important role to play in whatever we do in life.

Performing fairly well in the first two semesters of my MBA, I had kept my interest alive in sports and continued to be in the university Cricket team and Campus Table Tennis team. I, however, did not allow my love for sports to affect my studies most of the time, though at times it was inevitable.

Earlier, when the result of the first semester was declared, I secured 89 out of 100 marks in one of the written papers on Organisational Behaviour-I, which was the highest in the class. But I was shocked to find that in the internal assessment by the teacher, I was assessed only for 15 out of 25 marks.

Since it was a small class of 20, I also came to know that all the other nineteen students were assessed between 18 to 22 marks. Dismayed, I went to the professor with my mark sheet and respectfully inquired about the basis for assessing me at the lowest rung in the class.

After having a look at my marks sheet, the teacher appeared a bit apologetic, but the explanation given by him was rather startling. He told me that he often saw me playing cricket or table tennis during his evening walks and occasional visits to the Boys' Hostel. This made him assume that I was a "sportsman type" of a student, who was not very keen on studies! I had hardly come across a funnier explanation from a senior university teacher.

I pleaded with him that he should have assessed me on the basis of my performance in the class. I also told him that he should have appreciated that one of his good students was a fairly good sportsman as well. He, however, made amends while assessing me in the Organisation Behaviour –II paper in the second semester and did not hold my additional quality of being a sportsman against me.

During the second semester, something very interesting happened that changed the course of my career. As I got back to my hostel cubicle after attending the classes, one of my close friends and hostel-mates, Ashu Gupta, who was pursuing an M. Phil in Chemistry, came to my room and asked me to lend fifty rupees to him, which I did.

After a few days, he came back to me and returned fifteen rupees or so, along with the receipt of a registered letter and a counterfoil of a postal order for twenty-eight rupees, sent by him to the Union Public Service Commission (UPSC). A bit confused, I looked at him quizzically.

❦ ❦ ❦

I was still gaping at his face after Ashu told me that he had signed the application for me and picked up my passport-size photographs from my cupboard. I could not believe that he would do something so unusual.

Evidently, his intention was to prepare and appear for the CDS examination together, prepare for the Services Selection Board (SSB) interview along with me, and eventually pass out together as officers from the Officers' Training School (OTS) Madras (now Chennai). Later, in the year 1988, OTS was renamed as Officers' Training Academy (OTA).

Ashu also reminded me that Jatish Sharma, another common friend and my former classmate in MBA, had also left the course a few weeks ago after his selection to join the training at the OTS.

The idea of preparing for an exam without actually applying for it sounded quite ridiculous to me. I had known from the very beginning that Ashu was very keen to join the Army and had unsuccessfully appeared for the SSB interview once earlier. I did not want to disappoint him with my strong objection to what he had done. So, I decided to keep quiet, as there was no harm in appearing for the exam.

One evening, while I was preparing for the examination with Ashu, a strange incident took place. Another close friend, Vivek Kaul, who was preparing for the civil services examination and had his cubicle on the same floor of the hostel as mine, came to my room and did something outlandish. He threw a thick General Knowledge Digest in front of me and said, "Shekhar, ask anything from anywhere in this book."

I was astounded. "Anything, from anywhere? You mean out of the WHOLE book?" I reconfirmed, unbelievingly looking at the 600-odd page digest.

"Yes, the whole book," Vivek replied confidently.

I asked him several questions from various sections of the book, answers to many of which were not known to me. But he stumped me by answering all the questions correctly. This incident motivated me not only to prepare hard for the CDS examination but also for the civil services examination later.

After a year, Vivek Kaul cracked the Himachal State Administrative Services and joined a Class-I service of the State. He followed it up after a couple of years with his selection in the Indian Postal Services (Group-A service under the UPSC civil services examination). He later retired as Chief Post Master General of an Indian State before joining the corporate sector at the top management level.

The SSB Interview

A couple of months later, both Ashu and I appeared for the CDS exam, qualified, and received calls for interviews in July 1978. I was required to appear at SSB Bhopal for the interview, and Ashu's interview was scheduled on the same day at SSB Allahabad. As expected, Ashu was quite ecstatic about it, and almost every day, for hours together, he would discuss with me the strategy to succeed in the forthcoming interviews.

Three days before the scheduled date of the interviews, both of us left for our respective native places to proceed further to our interview destinations from there. As expected, the SSB interview was quite comprehensive and lasted four days. It tested all the candidates thoroughly in several qualities like leadership, intelligence, reasoning, physical fitness, teamwork, and psychometric suitability, etc.

A notable incident took place during the course of the interview which is worth narrating here. Among many ground tests, there was an obstacle test consisting of 10 obstacles numbered from 1 to 10, each containing the same number of marks as their respective serial numbers. It obviously meant that the numbering of the obstacles from 1 to 10 was done in ascending order of the level of difficulty of the obstacle concerned. In other words, obstacle No. 10, the toughest one, carried 10 marks, No. 9 was assigned 9 and so on, with a total of 55 marks for the entire test.

One could start attempting the obstacles from any obstacle of one's choice. However, a unique feature of the obstacle test was that if one completed the entire obstacle test before the assigned time, one could repeat some of the obstacles in the remaining time and would get additional marks for the repeated obstacles. In other words, a candidate could score more than 100 per cent marks in that test.

There was a candidate with us who was very agile and physically fit. Most of us in the group could complete 8 or 9 obstacles within the assigned one-minute time. Interestingly, that gentleman completed all ten obstacles with several seconds to spare and repeated three obstacles numbered from 8 to 10, meaning that he obtained 82 against 55 marks in the test. His performance in a few other tasks aimed at testing physical fitness was equally good.

On the fourth day before the final result was announced, the last part of the selection process took place. During the final event known as the "Conference," all three members of the selection board, i.e. the Chairman, the Group Testing Officer (GTO), and the Psychologist sat together to compile their assessment and jointly meet every candidate for a couple of minutes before the selections were finalised and announced.

While announcing the result, the GTO clarified that the defence forces looked for some specific qualities in the candidates and any candidate who was not selected should not consider himself as "not good enough". The GTO also informed that such candidates could be more suitable for other services like the civil services or managerial jobs and need not be disheartened.

He quoted a few instances when the candidates who could not qualify the SSB interview later did very well in life by getting selected for the civil services or joining as executives in some prestigious corporate entities.

GTO then announced the selections. In our batch of 30, three of us were selected. Most of us had expected that the gentleman, who had obtained 82 marks in the obstacle test, would get selected, as he had displayed marked superiority of his physical fitness over all of us in many of the other ground tests as well. At the same time, in many other tests like group planning, group discussion, lecturette, & teamwork tasks etc, his performance could have been better. But to our surprise, in the final list, the name of the said gentleman was missing!

Immediately after the result was announced, all those who could not make it were asked to pack their baggage and proceed to the railway station to catch the next available train for their return journeys.

After the unsuccessful candidates had left the hall, one of us asked the GTO for the reason for not selecting the candidate who repeated three obstacles, despite being so fit. The reply of the GTO was so amusing that I still remember every word of it.

"No doubt, physically he was in perfect shape," the GTO replied, "but his performance in the group tasks, psychometric tests and the Chairman's interview was found lacking. He also lacked the leadership qualities required for becoming an Army officer. We look for candidates who possess most of the required personality traits."

Then he paused for a while and said, "In a lighter vein, the defence forces need officers and not just monkeys."

Out of our complete batch in three separate groups, seven candidates were selected under three different GTOs. The selected candidates were required to appear before a medical board after some additional documentation. Over the next 5 days, all seven of us appeared for a comprehensive medical examination at the Military Hospital (MH).

Except for one candidate, who was temporarily rejected and was asked to come back for re-examination after one month, the rest of us were declared medically fit. The next day, I left Bhopal and reached my native place and spent a day with my parents before proceeding to Shimla to join my classes at the university campus.

I was very keen to know the outcome of my friend Ashu's interview. I met him in his hostel room in the evening and was shell-shocked when he told me that at the last minute, he had decided not to go for the interview! It was unbelievable!!

He then explained to me that his parents had argued with him that with his skinny frame, it might not be possible for him to complete the tough Army training successfully. They could not convince him, and he finally decided against going for the interview.

Initially, I was not very keen to join the OTS and wanted to complete my MBA degree. But at the same time, I also wanted to settle earlier in my career. Moreover, it was a short service commission, and I would have the option to leave after getting the enriching experience of serving in the Indian Army. Though it was a difficult decision, considering everything in totality, I decided to wait for the call and join.

But then there was yet another unexpected hiccup. At the beginning of October, another student at the universitycampus who had also qualified for the SSB for the same short service course received his call letter to join the training at the OTS and was required to be there by the 20th of October.

I waited and waited but did not receive any call until the 15th October, and it started to get frustrating. It was on the 16th October that I received a telephonic call on the hostel landline from my father who informed me that a letter was received addressed to me from the OTS Madras. I requested him to open the cover and read it for me.

My father read the letter to me. The letter was from the officer in charge of the CSD canteen at the OTS and read as follows:

"Dear Candidate,

This is to inform you that adequate quantities of the swimming trunks are available at the CSD canteen at the OTS Madras at reasonable prices. So, when you come to join the training, you need not carry a swimming trunk with you and can purchase it here.

Signed
Officer in Charge
CSD, OTS Madras."

The letter made it more than evident that a call letter was issued to me, but somehow I had not received it. Something was required to be done urgently, and I decided to visit the Army HQ. But I didn't even know which branch of the Army HQ looked after the OTS training.

One of my relatives was serving as a Major in the Corps of Engineers in the Army and was posted in Calcutta. I got his phone number and discussed the issue with him over the phone. He told me that the matter was looked after by the Adjutant General (AG) Branch of the Army HQ located at R K Puram, New Delhi, and asked me to visit the concerned office. He also gave me the room number and the landline details of one of his batch=mates, Major Nitin, posted in that branch, assuring me that by the time I reached there, he would have spoken to him.

Taking a night bus to Delhi, I reached the said office the very next morning and met the said officer. Major Nitin called the concerned civilian staff officer and asked him to check why I did not receive the call letter for training. After going through the office record, what came to light was very amusing.

It was revealed that the call letter was issued to me along with other selected candidates. It was addressed to my permanent address of Bilaspur (HP). But while recording my address on the dispatch register, instead of writing HP, the word MP was written erroneously.

The dispatch clerk seemingly made the same mistake while copying my address from the register to the envelope. Consequently, the call letter, instead of reaching me, travelled to Bilaspur in Madhya Pradesh. Chhattisgarh was not carved out as a separate state until then, and Bilaspur of modern-day Chhattisgarh was part of united Madhya Pradesh at that time. Furthermore, the Postal Index Number (PIN) did not exist at that time to cross-check the exact address location.

But all is well that ends well. A duplicate call letter was issued the same day and given to me by hand to join the OTS on or before 7th November. A few other candidates who had requested an extension to join were also given the same date to do so. Before leaving Delhi, I went to New Delhi Railway Station to book a seat to Madras. The earliest train seat available from Delhi to Madras was on the Tamil Nadu Express leaving on the evening of 3rd November, which I booked before catching a night bus for my return journey.

It was ironic that my friend Ashu, who was very keen to join the Army, dithered at the last moment and missed the opportunity to fulfil his childhood dream, while I ended up for training at OTS. This happened despite the fact that joining the Army was not on my career radar until a few months ago, and I did not even apply for the examination! For me, destiny perhaps played its part through Ashu as its agent.

Before I left the university to join the OTS, several friends and teachers tried to convince me that joining the Army may not be a good idea, as I was already towards the end of the third semester of my MBA and after a few months, I was expected to get a cushy managerial job. But I had already taken the decision. In retrospect, I feel that joining the Indian Army was among the best decisions that I made in my life.

Though I left the Army after about six years without pursuing a career there, the experience and exposure I gained during those six years left an indelible mark on my personality. The unique training, the exotic locations across the country, the adventurous missions, and the vibrant social life of the Army cannot be experienced except by being there. I was fortunate to get that exposure early in my career.

Chapter-VII

"Sweat More In Peace-Bleed Less In War"

'We don't rise to the level of our expectations, we fall to the level of our training'

—A famous quote

The euphoria of joining Army training suddenly seemed to vanish. This certainly was not the way I expected to be treated at the OTS. With the entire weight of my body on my arms, both my hands on the floor and both my legs resting high on the wall and pointing towards the roof of the barber shop, I could turn my head and see the trainee officers of the senior course sitting on a bench and waiting for their turn for a haircut.

❧ ❧ ❧

It was on a Sunday, 5th November 1978. I disembarked from the Tamil Nadu Express at Madras Central railway station early in the morning. I, along with six others, was received and picked up by a JCO in a military truck and escorted to the OTS located at St Thomas Mount near Guindy. I was excitedly anxious about the idea of starting my professional career.

Notwithstanding the anxiety, I felt a bit reassured on two counts. Firstly, Jatish Sharma, my friend and classmate in MBA, was already undergoing training in the second term. Secondly, another friend and schoolmate of mine, Rakesh, was also there in the senior term.

As all seven of us got down from the vehicle at the main gate of the OTS, in a cabin next to the gate, we were asked to make an entry in a register with one instructor named Captain Mukesh Kapoor. After making the entries, we were assigned our respective GC (Gentleman Cadet) numbers. We were also informed that we were part of the SS-28 course.

In about 15 minutes, we were done with the arrival rituals. Captain Kapoor made us pick up our steel trunks and bedding hold-alls and asked us to proceed to our respective barracks, which were a few hundred metres away. It was the first test of endurance for all of us.

Welcome to the OTS, Shekhar!

As guided by the instructor, all of us reported to the barracks of Ranjit Singh (RS) Battalion, Kohima Company, platoon No. 18 (K-18), where a group of seniors was eagerly waiting for us. For the next about half an hour, we were made to do many awkward things in the name of 'introduction'.

During the 'introduction', some of the 'rules' were spelled out to us by the seniors. While in our first term, we were expected to be jogging in a troop formation, while moving from place A to place B. The OTS cafeteria was "out of bounds" for the junior course. Further, we were advised to take at least 15 glasses of water with some added salt daily to avoid dehydration to survive in the sultry weather. Another rule was that the junior course GCs were supposed to keep their moustaches shaved off during the entire first term.

After the broad 'rules' were spelled out to us, all of us were also asked to shave off our moustaches immediately, to be followed by a 'proper' haircut later. All seven of us immediately rushed to the toilets, shaved off our moustaches and then hurriedly jogged in a group to the barber shop nearby.

At the barber shop, we were greeted by a few more enthusiastic seniors who were waiting for their turn for the weekly haircuts. One of the seniors present there asked us to take an "easy position" while waiting for our turn. All of us gave a blank look as we were not aware of what an easy position was.

"You bloody clowns, you don't even know what an easy position is?" shouted another one.

He then described it to us, and all of us followed the description. The very next moment, along with others, I found myself on my hands upside down against the wall! Through my two arms, I looked at a few seniors sitting on the bench, unsuccessfully searching for Jatish or Rakesh to come to my rescue.

The next half an hour was terrible. The hot and humid Madras made all of us sweat profusely. With about 10 barber cabins in the shop, all the seniors were done in about half an hour, and we could take the luxury of sitting on the benches while waiting for our turn.

After the haircut, with no moustache and virtually a zero-cut hair on my head, I looked like a stranger to myself in the mirror. With a similar haircut and devoid of moustaches, all of us looked alike from a distance. Thereafter, wherever we saw any GC with a moustache, he was assumed to be from the senior course and we would stretch both our arms straight down and wish him loudly

Initial Days

Later in the day, we were issued a few pairs of shorts, vests, socks, rain capes, and a few sets of uniforms & overalls. We were also assigned one bed in a large barracks, along with a study table and a steel cupboard each.

A tailor came to our barracks in the evening and took measurements for mufti pants, white shirts, and a white patrol. Mufti was the official and formal civilian outfit to be worn for dinners or for outings on holidays. It consisted of a pair of light grey pants, a white shirt, an OTS tie, black Oxford Pattern (OP) shoes, a pair of black socks, and a white handkerchief in the pocket.

White Patrol, on the other hand, is a pair of white trousers and a jacket with metallic glossy buttons, required to be worn during the formal dinner nights. Until the mufti and white patrol were stitched, we were asked to wear our own trousers with a white shirt, OP shoes, and OTS tie for dinner nights.

The initial few weeks at the OTS seemed very strenuous. We were required to wake up at 0515 hrs in the morning, go for two hours of tough physical training (PT) at 0600 hrs, have breakfast at 0830 hrs and then go for pre-lunch sessions lasting about five hours, which included the march-past drills, obstacle course training, weapon training, map reading, shooting, tactics and some academics like Hindi, English, Military History, Geography etc.

After a brief post-lunch break, we were expected to go for organised sports lasting two hours. The emphasis during the sports period was on 'troop games' like football, hockey, basketball, volleyball, etc. 'Officer games' like cricket, table tennis, lawn tennis, etc. were also available but only occasionally.

A quick bath after the games was followed by a mandatory study period from 1830 hrs to 1930 hrs. We were then expected to be in the GCs' mess for dinner before 2000 hrs. Dinners were like yet another parade for the junior course. With the seniors sharing the same dining tables, we were taught the correct use of cutlery, table etiquette, and mess decorum in detail.

All Mondays were dinner night days, denoting the formal dinners in white patrol. As the name suggests, such dinner nights were aimed at acquainting the GCs with the procedure to be followed in the 'guest dinners' later in service. In a dinner night, one of the officers would be the 'guest' and the dinner would begin only the moment the 'guest' would start eating. Everyone was supposed to stop eating and close one's plate the moment the 'guest' did so.

Dinners would generally be over before 2100 hrs. Regardless of whether the dinner was formal or informal, the junior course GCs were required to sit upright on the chairs in the mess throughout and were never permitted to rest their elbows on the table. After dinner, there would invariably be 'fall-ins' by the senior course appointment holders, where we had to endure about an hour of tough exercises as per the diktats of the seniors, also called *'Ragda'* in a lighter vein. We would then return to our barracks and be in our beds before the 'lights out' time.

A sudden increase in physical activity seemed very exhausting during the first few weeks. To make things worse, the additional grinding by the seniors was also very frequent. During the entire first term, physical toil ranged from 6 to 7 hours daily, because of which, despite the very sumptuous food served in the mess, we would start feeling starved hours before the next meal.

More particularly in the evenings, we would begin to have strong pangs of hunger after the games period. The only option was the cafeteria, but the juniors were not permitted there. My friend Rakesh, however, would invariably come to my barracks at around 6 PM almost every day, carrying some snacks for me from the canteen.

In the humid heat of Madras while jogging from place A to place B, one would come across a befitting slogan written on several walls - "Sweat more in peace, Bleed less in war". In a single sentence, this slogan described the very purpose of a strenuous training schedule. Appearing more than once daily before our eyes, the slogan kept us all motivated to put in our best.

The duration of the first term was about 5 months. In addition to qualifying various tests like the PT, marching drills, weapon handling & shooting, a few academic papers, map reading, miscellaneous tests and obstacle course, we were also required to pass 2-mile and 10-mile races in battle dress with excellent timings. Captain Arman Contractor, an outstanding officer of the Corps of Engineers, was the Directing Staff (DS) for our platoon, who later rose to the rank of a Brigadier.

Daily PT classes were very exhausting, and the PT tests were even tougher to qualify for. PT tests included dozens of push-ups and sit-ups, several pull-ups on a bar and a wooden beam, a one-mile run, a vertical and a horizontal wooden horse jump, a vertical rope climb etc., to name a few.

Handling of small arms with proficiency and passing the shooting skills test with weapons like rifles, light machine guns, carbines, and pistols were a few other tests to be qualified. Two hours were devoted daily to marching drills practice, and the GCs were tested in drill proficiency every 2-3 weeks. For non-swimmers and weak swimmers, there were special coaching classes in the swimming pool after lunch.

Generally speaking, the training in the OTS was arguably more strenuous than that in the Indian Military Academy (IMA). The reason was that the curriculum of the pre-commission training, which was required to be completed in 18 months in the IMA, had to be completed in about 10 months in the OTS.

A Proxy for Test

The training was so arduously designed that the tests, which seemed formidable in the first two weeks, seemed easier to pass later. During the initial few weeks, most of us lost several kilograms of weight, part of which was recovered later when the muscle mass started to build up.

Many of us would find one or the other test too difficult to qualify. One such example was the pull-ups on a high beam which many trainees could not do initially, but gradually as the training progressed, it seemed relatively facile. One of my course-mates, a platoon fellow and a dear friend, Anil Ghaira, who apparently seemed to have a very good physique, found the high beam extremely difficult. He failed to perform even a single pull-up in the first beam test and flunked.

Before the retest was scheduled after a couple of weeks, I would take Ghaira to the PT ground before going to bed at night and make him practice by supporting his body with both my hands, but to his frustration, he was just not able to pull his body up even once.

It was obvious that if he did not pass the test in the coming weeks, he was sure to face the risk of relegation to the junior course, which meant repeating the first term all over again. In addition, he had to face the stigma of being called a 'relegated type' throughout the entire term.

On the eve of his retest, I took Anil to the PT ground after dinner. While practising , it was the same story again as he failed to pull his body weight up to the beam. I could see tears in his eyes when he said, "Shekhar, I think I will never be able to pass the beam." I tried to encourage him, but Anil himself was not sure whether he would ever be able to qualify.

It was at that moment when I decided to help him with something bizarre. I offered to take the test for him by faking my identity as Anil Ghaira. He was initially hesitant and told me that it would be unethical. But on second thought, he agreed.

Both of us knew that it involved a great risk for both of us. If we were caught, both were certain to be relegated to the next junior course for 'utter lack of officer-like qualities'. But at that age, perhaps it seemed more important to help a friend than to bother about the ethics or the consequences.

We mutually decided on the modus operandi. Out of 30-odd cadets in our platoon, twelve GCs had failed in their first attempt. We were in the initial two months of training and in a batch of 285, the PT *ustaads* were not yet familiar with the names of most of us. Moreover, with a similar haircut and PT dress, everyone looked similar. So, the risk of being caught was minimal.

The next day, the GC numbers of all twelve GCs required to take the test were called one by one by the PT *ustad*. When Ghaira's GC number was called out, I stepped out without any hesitation. The entire platoon witnessing the test knew that I was acting as Ghaira's proxy, but everyone maintained a poker face as if nothing unusual was happening. I meticulously did the required number of pull-ups on the beam, and Anil Ghaira was declared to have passed the test!

When I look back in retrospect, I realise that what we both did was extremely brazen, unethical and immature. In all probability, Ghaira would have passed the test on his own after a few weeks because at the end of the term, all those who had failed in the first attempt could manage to qualify the beam test easily. It was one of the foolish acts of the young age.

A Bout to Remember!

Boxing was a compulsory sport, and all of us were supposed to participate in the OTS boxing championship. The purpose was to inculcate the so-called "killing instinct" among all the prospective officers. This was one of the sports with which I was not familiar. After a couple of days of basic training, I was pushed into the ring for a formal fight.

I was pitted against Sunil Chauhan, my platoon mate and a close friend, who also hailed from Himachal Pradesh. Chauhan was two inches taller than me and a bit heavier too. To my bad luck, Sunil had been a college boxing champion in his weight. Despite two days of coaching and my sincere attempts to put up a good fight by landing a few punches on Chauhan's face, I got knocked out in the second round after taking a few nasty blows on my nose.

Ups and Downs

My friends Jatish and Rakesh would often come to me in the evenings to encourage me to do well in my training. Jatish himself was doing extremely well and had earned the highest cadet appointment of School Cadet Adjutant (SCA). The cadet appointments were given in the second term to meritorious cadets based on their overall performance in all the tests including PT, drill, academics, map reading, weapon training, tactics, and most importantly the "officer-like qualities" (OLQs).

Later, Jatish graduated from the academy as the top student of the SS-27 course and was awarded the "Sword of Honour" for being an all-round best cadet. He also won the gold medal for being the best in academics in his batch. He had the privilege of commanding the passing out parade on 17th March 1979 and received the sword and the gold medal from the chief guest during the parade.

Along with Jatish, Rakesh also passed out with flying colours. In addition to these two friends in the senior course, I made some very good friends with many of my own course mates.

A few other incidents that left a lasting impression on me are vivid in my mind even today. One such incident is the death of one of my training mates, G. K. Mohandas. While running the 10-mile race on a hot and humid day, Mohandas collapsed 50 metres short of the finish line due to extreme dehydration. He was immediately air-lifted to the Command Hospital Air Force, Bangalore, in a critical condition, where he breathed his last after a few hours.

The tragic news of the demise of Mohandas spelled gloom among all the GCs. Sensing the negative sentiment among the cadets, the Commandant of the academy addressed both the courses that evening, wherein he tried to lift up everyone's spirits. He tried to press home the point that if we had chosen the Army as a career, we had to be mentally prepared to occasionally lose our colleagues during the course of our careers, more so during the operations.

For one of the map-reading exercises, I was nominated as the platoon commander by the DS. As a platoon leader, I was required to lead the platoon to march to a given destination, which was about 15 kilometres away. The task required me to guide my men to the finish point by reading the given map and using a compass at night. Before we set off, Captain Arman Contractor cautioned us not to cross River Adiyar and to remain on its right bank all through the route.

One was expected to mark the direction to the destination on the map, check the angle and distance from own position and set the bearing of that angle on the compass. For measuring the ground distance while walking, one GC was deputed to assist, who was responsible for counting the steps and converting those steps into metres, as per the training imparted.

While going strictly by the compass bearing, at one point I faced a dilemma. There was a place where the route suggested by the compass bearing required us to cross a wide, dry, and sandy trench. Before crossing over to the other side, I had a strong hunch that it was the river, but many of the platoon mates argued that the dry and sandy trench could not be Adiyar, and a majority decision was taken to continue exactly as per the compass, and we crossed the 'trench'.

But after walking another mile, we found ourselves on the wrong side of the river, which, beyond that point, was full of deep water. That's when we realised that the dry canal we crossed earlier was actually the river. Some of my platoon mates were badly tired and openly began to criticise me for making them walk extra kilometres, for which they later apologised.

Most of us were not aware that many smaller South Indian rivers are not perennial in nature, and that ignorance on the part of most of us made us take a wrong decision. After walking another three kilometres, we could find a bridge to cross over to the right side and get back on track. In the bargain, we had to walk a few extra kilometres.

In the process, I learned a great lesson. For any decision taken as a leader, one shall always remain responsible, even if the decision was taken by a general consensus. Further, as a leader, whenever in doubt due to insufficient information, one must go by one's hunch.

The Interview Call

One evening, after I got back from the games period, I received a letter re-directed to me from my university hostel address. It contained an interview call from the HP State Public Service Commission for selection to the State Civil Services.

Before joining the training at the OTS, I had appeared for the written exam without any specific preparation and did not expect to qualify. Receiving the interview call gave me an elated feeling that I had not only passed but was also shortlisted for the interview, even though the number of vacancies was small.

My interview was scheduled two weeks later in Shimla. I was aware that, as per the regulations, no leave was allowed to the GCs, except for the four-week term break after five months of training. That evening, I consulted Jatish and Rakesh, who suggested that I should seek an interview with the battalion commander and request a few days' casual leave, as a special case, to appear for the said interview.

Accordingly, I sought a formal interview with the battalion commander who was a Colonel from Maratha Light Infantry. During the interview, the battalion commander informed me that as per the rules under the Army Act, the GCs were neither allowed any leave, nor were permitted to appear for any civil job interviews. He also told me that if I was keen to go for the said interview, I had to resign from Army training after depositing the entire cost of my training. Those days, the cost of training was around forty thousand rupees. I requested the Colonel to allow me a day to think over it.

That night, I objectively considered the entire situation. I was already assured of a prestigious job in the Army as a commissioned officer after completion of training in another about six months. On the other side, the interview call for another coveted civil job was just a call, and there was no certainty that I would finally be selected. Moreover, forty thousand rupees was a huge sum in those days, and even if my father somehow managed to remit the cost of my training, the result of the interview would still be uncertain.

After considering all the aspects, I decided to continue with my Army training at the OTS. Later, on completion of the training, when we were allowed 28 days' leave before joining as officers, I visited the State Public Service Commission office in Shimla to obtain my detailed marks card. The office superintendent, while handing over the card to me, was surprised that I was marked as "Absent" in the interview. He told me that the marks obtained by me were among the highest in the exam and had I attended the interview, I stood a very good chance of getting selected.

At that instance, I remembered Ashu Gupta, my friend at the university who had filled up my application form for the CDS examination. Becoming an Army officer at the beginning of my career was perhaps my fate, and I was not destined to join the civil services at that stage.

In Pursuit of a Parantha

All the GCs who qualified the marching drill proficiency test were allowed to get an 'out pass' to go to Madras City on Sundays for a 6-hour outing. I remember that after passing my drill test, I went out on my first outpass with five more friends. We all desperately wanted to eat *Paranthas*. Food in the OTS mess provided us with almost all types of dishes including English, Continental, Chinese, South Indian, North Indian, and Mughlai. The only item missing on the menu was a *Parantha* for breakfast.

That day we searched the entire Mount Road market and visited a few restaurants looking for our favourite dish. After several unsuccessful attempts, we could locate the item on the menu of a posh restaurant named Impala. Excitedly, we ordered one piece each. But to our dismay, what we were actually served was a plain crispy Chilla-type dish prepared with rice flour and served with *Sambar*, which tasted more like a Dosa!

This initial setback did not deter us. On the following Sunday, we continued with our quest on the sub-lanes of Mount Road and could finally see a signboard, with "Sher-e-Punjab" written outside a small restaurant, which looked more like a *Dhaba*. Excitedly, we moved closer and found a Sikh youth sitting at the counter. We immediately knew that our quest for the coveted Punjabi dish was finally over.

We entered the *Dhaba* and ordered two *Pranthas* each with curd and butter. One of our Punjabi friends, Sanjiv Chatyal, asked the young Sardarji in Punjabi how he felt being in South India. We were flabbergasted when the young man replied in Tamil, *"Punjabi Illai"*, meaning that he could not speak Punjabi!

He then explained to us in English that he was born and brought up in Madras and could understand Punjabi, which was spoken by his parents and grandfather but was not able to speak the language. Coming from North India, it seemed quite inexplicable to us. Though the young man turned out to be a Tamilian Sikh, the *Paranthas* served to us were genuinely North Indian in taste.

Weekend Movies

There was an open-air theatre in the academy where, on the weekends, movies were exhibited for the trainee GCs and the staff, including the officers posted there. Every Saturday evening a Hindi movie was screened, while Sunday evenings came with a Hollywood one, generally a war or action movie. The open-air theatre had a white wall in front serving as the screen.

An auditorium was in the final stages of construction and became functional three months after my joining.

For watching the movies, the junior course GCs would sit on the chairs in the first few rows, followed by the senior course, and finally the staff and the officers with their families at the end. The staff enclosure at the rear was covered from the top.

Until the lights were switched off and the movie began, all the GCs were expected to sit on the chairs in attention mode, with their head and eyes in a straight position and arms stretched forward on the knees. To ensure a bit of privacy for the officers, staff, and their families, under no circumstances was any GC permitted to look backwards. Violation of this rule invited strict punishment.

It was mandatory for the trainees to be present for the movies. The dress code for the movies was mufti for the GCs. During the first three months of training, we watched the movies in the open-air theatre. Due to heavy winter rains in that area, we were required to carry our rain capes with us for the movies. I remember watching several movies in heavy rain with a rain cape over the mufti and the rainwater dripping inside, leaving us drenched.

On a Saturday, while watching a popular Hindi movie, some of the senior course GCs snapped their fingers in unison for a few seconds along with the rhythm of a popular song. It was noticed by the Adjutant of the academy, who was also watching the movie. During the interval break, the Adjutant came in front, scolded all the GCs for displaying gross indiscipline and ordered everyone to remain seated after the movie.

As the film ended, the entire staff and families left. The Adjutant again came forward, gave a moral lecture for a few minutes and then personally supervised a strenuous *Ragada* as punishment to all the GC for about an hour. Later, when we went to the mess for dinner, we were all completely soaked in sweat and sand.

Though one of the formal teachings imparted to the trainee officers in the academy was to avoid mass punishment of the subordinate troops, it was more than once that we were all subjected to collective comeuppance during the 10-month training. And this was one such incident, the intent of which perhaps was to instil a sense of discipline among us.

Extra-Curricular

Regular games in the evenings helped me acquire good expertise in some troop games like basketball, football, and hockey, which I had not played seriously in my college days. Furthermore, I was picked up for 400-metre and 800-metre races for my training battalion team. Based on my performance in the inter-company cricket tournament in the OTS, I was also named for the academy cricket team.

The exhilaration of the above selection was, however, short-lived. On the following evening, Captain Chakku, the officer in charge of the cricket team, informed us that an inter-academy sports tournament was to be held at the Indian Military Academy (IMA) in Dehradun during the fourth week of March. He also told us that the selected ones would participate in the said tournament and miss their mid-term break.

It was shocking to learn, as I was eagerly looking forward to the break. So were my parents, who were also eager to see me, as I could make out from their letters. But that was not to be. I informed my family through a letter, and they were equally disappointed.

The last event before the term break was 'Nomad'. Nomad was a 120-kilometre route march exercise in 'battle order', to be completed in two and a half days. The march seemed quite challenging to brave through the sultry summer of Madras. The excitement of getting over with the first term helped most of us to endure it successfully. Immediately after Nomad and just before our term break, the senior course passed out as officers, and we got promoted to the senior course, ready to welcome our juniors after the term break.

As the mid-term break commenced for the rest of the course, I, along with a few others, had to stay back and prepare for the impending triangular sports meet at IMA Dehradun. After a week's practice and preparations, we left for Dehradun.

We were given accommodation at the IMA campus. During the next week, we played a few matches. The hockey, football, and athletics teams also participated. All the OTS teams did well, and the cricket team secured the second position in the meet.

On the last day of the tournament, my parents gave me a pleasant surprise by arriving in Dehradun to see me. Our return journey to Madras was after four days. So, my father requested Major Rayudu, the officer in charge of the OTS contingent, to allow him to take me home for a couple of days. Major Rayudu was kind enough to agree on the condition that on the return journey day, I must reach New Delhi Railway Station in the afternoon and join the entire group for its return journey.

I had just about a day and a half at home. The unexpected short vacation at home after 5 months of rigorous training was thoroughly enjoyable. I could see many friends and near & dear ones before catching up with the rest of the group at New Delhi Railway Station on the journey day.

The Senior Term

After we reached Madras, the term break ended after a few days, marking the beginning of the second term of training. Based on my performance during the first term, I was given the appointment of Platoon Under-Officer (PUO).

Soon thereafter, the GCs of the junior course SS-29 joined the training. Graduating to the role of seniors, we started mentoring the junior course GCs in the same manner as our seniors did to us.

The second term did not seem to be as gruelling as the first one; perhaps our bodies had got appropriately toned up with vigorous physical activity earlier. The training staff was more considerate towards us, and there was no pressure of close scrutiny by the seniors and their resultant *"Ragda"*.

Shocking Slashes

An incident worth narrating, related to the weekend movies, took place during the second term as well, this time in the newly constructed movie auditorium. On a Sunday, an English movie was to be screened for the entire academy. The officers and their families were also seated in the balcony meant for them. The dress code was "mufti" for all the GCs.

Earlier that day, most of the senior course GCs had got out passes and been to the city. It had rained heavily, and the mufti dress as well as the OP shoes of most of us got completely drenched. In the case of several GCs, including me, the second set of mufti had not been received back from the washer-man. Due to high humidity, the wet dress did not dry up even under the fan till evening, forcing many of the senior course GCs, including me, to wear civvies for the movie.

During the intermission, the academy Adjutant noticed that several GCs of the senior course were not 'properly dressed'. Before the movie resumed, he came in front of the screen and announced that after the movie, the senior course was required to stay back.

As the movie ended, all the officers and families, as well as the junior course GCs, left the auditorium. We could guess that some kind of punishment was on the anvil. But what actually happened was just ludicrous. The SCA, who was in mufti dress himself, on the instruction of the Adjutant, asked the entire senior course to fall in outside the auditorium. He carried out the headcount and reported to the Adjutant that the entire course was present.

The Adjutant came forward and asked a few who were dressed in mufti to step back. He then announced that coming for the movie in improper dress was not acceptable, as it was an act of sheer indiscipline. One GC named Nitin Malhotra tried to explain that the mufti set was too wet to be worn. Malhotra was punished with 50 front rolls for 'unnecessary argument'. The Adjutant reasoned that in case it was raining, we all could have skipped going to the city or carried our rain capes along, rather than not following the dress code for the movie.

The Adjutant then said that the punishment he was going to announce and execute would ensure that for the rest of our Army career, we would never even think of violating the prescribed dress code. It was more than obvious that something extraordinary was going to hit us.

He then took out a brand new shaving blade from his pocket and with his own hands, slashed the trousers of a few GCs vertically from knees downwards by making several cuts. Then he handed over the blade to the SCA, asking him to slash the trousers of the remaining GCs in a similar manner. After slashing all the trousers, those wearing civilian shoes were asked to remove the shoes, which were also slashed from the toes.

At that point in time, the punishment seemed grossly disproportionate to the offence, but later I realised that it was perhaps aimed at bringing home the point that being properly dressed for any occasion was an important aspect of Army discipline. If we, as 'would be officers', did not comply with the requirement of being properly dressed, how could we check our subordinates from indulging in any act of similar indiscipline?

Last, not the Least

As a weak swimmer, I, along with a few other GCs, was required to take swimming lessons at the swimming pool during our spare time after lunch thrice a week. Saturdays would involve going to one of the hobby clubs in the afternoon. One was required to choose one of the hobby clubs out of painting, riding, yoga, photography, angling, and shooting. I opted for the riding club and learned horse riding with a fair degree of proficiency, as I had always been fascinated by the horses and found horse riding to be great fun.

Towards the end of the second and final term, there was an exciting exercise called 'Chhachhro'. It consisted of three separate raids on three consecutive nights, for which the entire platoon was led by one of the GCs, nominated by the DS to do so. The nominated leader was required to carry out complete planning and preparation for the raid, issue verbal orders to the raiding party and execute it in a mock 'enemy area' as if it were a real operation.

Planning and conduct of the raid were expected to be as per the instructions imparted during the tactics classes. The task was given by the DS in the morning at around 0900 hrs, after which a sand model and a larger map of the area were required to be prepared, depicting the onward route, important features of the terrain including the hillocks, the rivers/*nalas*, the forests, the 'enemy' minefields, possible location of the 'enemy' protective patrols, the 'enemy' area to be raided, the route of withdrawal after the raid, etc.

The platoon leader was supposed to issue verbal orders at around 1700 hrs, and the departure of the raiding party was generally scheduled at around 2000 hrs after dinner. All the above preparations were keenly observed by the DS to assess the GCs for their OLQs.

In addition to detailed planning and issuance of verbal orders, a single raid involved 5 to 6 hours of navigation and walking, entering the 'enemy' area and conducting the raid as planned, before rushing back for about 2 to 3 hours to a designated rendezvous (RV). The distances for Chhachhro were kept in such a way that after every raid, the platoon generally reached the RV not before the early morning of the next day. The DS would remain with the raiding party throughout the exercise to observe and assess.

After completing one raid and reaching the "own area" in the morning, the task for the next raid was spelled out by the DS in his briefing, for which the preparation of the sand model, the map, and the verbal orders were required to be prepared by all the GCs throughout the day. Another GC was designated by the DS as the commander for the second raid.

The most torturous part of the exercise was that the platoon was required to accomplish the task of executing three back-to-back raids on three consecutive nights with perfection, despite being deprived of sleep. The instructor would also go through the same rigour but could perhaps find some time to relax during the day when the GCs were busy preparing for the next raid.

The first two raids went off well. For the final raid, I was nominated to lead, and the task was explained by the DS at

0800 hrs after we got back from the second one. Most of us were already exhausted after the previous two raids. Leading and conducting the third one as a commander was certainly an uphill task.

We prepared the sand model and the blow-up map earlier in the day. As I began preparing for the verbal orders in the afternoon, I asked the other platoon mates to refresh themselves with a nap. At 1700 hrs, I issued the verbal orders. After an early supper, we all started our march towards the objective.

The final raid required the entire platoon to walk about 23 kilometres, enter the 'enemy' area stealthily, raid a tank harbour with two troops of tanks (total 6 in number) after midnight and then rush back to an RV by withdrawing almost 10 kilometres.

Everything went off as planned. Undetected by the 'enemy', we could easily enter the 'enemy' tank harbour, were able to put the explosive charges on all the 'enemy' tanks and detonated the explosives. The DS indicated to me that the raid was executed successfully, as symbolically we were able to destroy all the 'enemy' tanks.

The next and final act was to withdraw and rush back to the designated RV. Soon the exultation of another successful raid died down, and the fatigue started catching up. The last ten kilometres to the RV seemed unending.

We reached the RV at about 0430 hrs in the morning. It was deep inside a reserve forest. All of us were completely exhausted after three sleepless and stressful nights. On reaching the camping location, I made the entire platoon fall in, carried out the headcount and made sure that all the weapons of my platoon mates were intact. Then I gave an "all okay" report to the DS, who then asked all of us to 'relax' until 0700 hours when the mechanical transport was to arrive to take us back to the OTS campus.

After we were allowed to take a break, all of us moved to the adjoining camping site. While removing my "battle order" dress, I was awestruck when I suddenly discovered that the very light pistol was missing from its holster on my waist!

The weapon was issued to me as a platoon commander in addition to a 9 mm carbine. A very light pistol is a large-bore handgun that fires larger cartridges, discharging coloured flares and smoke. This type of gun is used to signal the successful completion of a mission to the seniors located far away by firing "red over green" shots in the sky. Loss of a weapon during training invited a minimum punishment of relegation to the junior course.

The loss of the pistol left me feeling extremely jittery. I distinctly remembered that I had checked the weapon in my holster about two kilometres short of our camping site. I was thus certain that it was in the last two kilometres of our walk back to the RV that it inadvertently slipped out of the holster hanging on my belt.

I looked around at my platoon mates, hoping to find someone who could assist me in the hopeless search. But by that time, most of them seemed dead tired and had fallen asleep. A few who were still awake appeared to be relieved that a long and gruelling exercise was finally over. Most of those who were still awake seemed reluctant to get moving again. As a big relief to me, two of my platoon mates, namely Sanjiv Chatiyal and Kapil Tyagi, offered to accompany me.

We went back on the same track as we had followed while coming to the camping area. During the wee hours, the search for a small pistol in the huge forest area with thick undergrowth was like a desperate search for a needle in a haystack. I could foresee my relegation to the junior course and visualised myself undergoing every test and exercise all over again, in addition to going back in my career by five months.

We searched for the weapon for about half an hour in vain. I had started losing hope when I heard Sanjiv call from behind, "Shekhar, let us go back and inform the DS about the loss of the weapon. I don't think we can find it now. You better be prepared for five extra months of training."

A positive note of excitement in his voice, however, told me a different story. And then, in the fading darkness of the night, I could see the pistol in his hand as he and Tyagi drew closer to me. Sanjiv told me that he found it under the thick cover of the bushes beside the path that we had followed earlier. I hugged both of them tightly and thanked them for their help despite being completely exhausted. It was camaraderie at its very best!

The Passing Out Parade

The second term was at its fag end. The last phase of the second term training involved the preparations for the ultimate event, the 'passing out parade' (PoP). The last few days thus involved long hours of marching drills and PoP rehearsals.

Several weeks before the PoP, all the cadets were asked about their options to choose the corps, regiment or battalion. Efforts were made by the Army HQ to allocate the corps or regiment of one's choice, but for obvious reasons, the choices of the majority of the GCs could not be honoured.

Top 5 per cent of the GCs in the final order of merit were termed to be in the "super block". All those who passed out in the "super block" were invariably commissioned into the arm, the service or the regiment of their choice in the Army. In a batch of 285, I passed out in 12th position and being in the "super block", I had the privilege of getting my choice.

I exercised my option for infantry in general and the Dogra Regiment in particular. A few days before the PoP, I was informed that I was to be commissioned in the 27th Battalion of the Dogra Regiment.

As per the regulations, the passing-out cadets could invite two of their relatives to witness the PoP, who were hosted by the academy. Accordingly, my younger brother Suneel and brother-in-law, Dr M. L. Mahajan, came to Madras to witness my passing out.

Finally, the day came for which we had slogged for ten months. Lieutenant General HN Seth presided over the parade as the chief guest. The parade went off well, and I passed out as a commissioned officer of the Indian Army on 1st September 1979.

Pre-commission training at the OTS was a great learning experience. A raw cadet is gradually turned into a trained Army leader within a short span of 10 months. Various aspects of training take care not only of the physical fitness of the cadets but also train them in marching drills, weapon handling, shooting, map reading, tactics of war, human resource management, etc. Furthermore, all the cadets must learn to play several sports and learn swimming.

General etiquette, table manners, communication skills, and respecting the ladies are some other attributes that enrich the personality of the cadets not only as Army officers but also as human beings. Whatever little I could achieve later in my life, I gratefully owe a large part of it to the Army training. That's the reason that many a time, I remember a famous tagline used by the Army to lure the youth to join as short service commissioned officers in the Army, which read as follows:

"Officers for five years, gentlemen for life"

Chapter-VIII

Raid and Attack

"Plans are worthless but planning is everything"
    –A famous Army quote often used
    by D. D. Eisenhower, a former US President

All of a sudden, a group of around 25 people armed with axes, shovels, sickles, and sticks attacked us from both sides of the road. The ambush took place on a narrow road through continuing rows of kutcha houses on both sides. What surprised me was that the offensive took place by maintaining complete surprise. It was well past 2300 hrs, and the dark night did help the assailants to attack us completely unnoticed.

☙ ☙ ☙

It happened on a cold January night in 1982 during an exercise by the Army Division, when we were crossing through a village. I was leading a patrol consisting of 12 soldiers when we encountered this unforeseen situation.

In 'peace' stations, during the winter months, the Army units are generally required to go out for exercises for a few weeks. Peace station exercises are the simulations of various operations of war in which the Army units carry out practical training in various military operations under the aegis of a brigade or a division/corps HQ.

During the division exercise that year, my unit was given the task of attacking the defences of an 'enemy' battalion near a village called Kashipore in West Bengal. I was assigned the exclusive task to lead a recce (reconnaissance) patrol in advance, move closer to the enemy defences stealthily, and reconnoitre the enemy defences in detail. More specifically, as the patrol commander, my task was to gather detailed information about the strength and deployment of the enemy troops and weapons.

After collecting the information, I was required to pass it on to the CO through coded wireless messages at least a day before a full-fledged attack was to be launched on the 'enemy' defences. An additional and more challenging task given to me as patrol commander was to raid the battalion HQ of the said enemy unit about half an hour before the main attack.

Since I would have seen the entire enemy area while gathering the information, it would be easier for me to conduct such a raid. The broader aim of the raid was to put the enemy command and control systems in disarray just before a full-fledged attack was launched.

My patrol party consisted of one section, i.e. 10 *Sepoys* including an NCO of the rank of *Naik* and one additional *Sepoy* from the signal platoon with a long-range radio wireless set for staying in touch with the unit. The rest of the battalion was to move a day after our departure.

Four days before the date of the attack, my detachment was transported by an Army vehicle to a point which was about 75 kilometres north-east of Ranchi. From the debussing point, we were required to enter the enemy area by walking a distance of about 60 kilometres in two days. We carried our service weapons with ammunition, along with sufficient quantities of dry rations and were self-contained for 4 days. Once the first task assigned to the patrol was accomplished, we were required to catch up with the battalion on the D-day (day of the attack), a few hours before carrying out our second task.

We began our march towards Kashipore at about 1000 hrs. I allocated the responsibilities of map reading, navigation, and security to four individuals from my team.

On day one, we covered almost 35 kilometres before deciding to halt for the night near a village. All of us were virtually famished, as we had not eaten proper meals after breakfast and managed only with a couple of bananas each and some tea. Two of the boys cooked rice and dal for dinner, and we ate huge portions before retiring to sleep under a big tree. Groups of two soldiers each guarded us in four shifts of two hours each.

Even during the end of January, the days had turned quite warm, but the nights were still cold. Being tired of walking for almost the whole day, we had a sound sleep to get re-energised for facing yet another tough day ahead.

The next day was equally challenging as we were to enter the 'enemy area' later during the day. A few snipers and hostile patrols were expected near the 'border' whom we were supposed to bypass.

Our aim was to get closer to Kashipore that evening by covering the remaining distance, as that would leave us with enough time to reconnoitre the enemy defences and gather maximum information on the third day and the night following that.

As the lunch was to be missed once again, we ate *Paranthas* for breakfast before setting off. After a couple of hours of rapid march, we approached the 'international border' and started moving carefully to avoid any contact with the 'enemy' detachments. Any conflict with the 'enemy' would have compromised not only our movement but also the tasks assigned to us.

The afternoon had become pretty warm as we entered West Bengal and crossed *Jaypore* village. We had made good progress and were about to cross the "international border". Going further ahead under the cover of the dark night would effectively hide our movement from the enemy. So, we decided to rest for about a couple of hours in the afternoon under a thick shady tree.

It required us to walk through most of the night to ensure that we reached as close to the 'enemy' defences as possible before retiring to sleep. We had decided to have dinner only after reaching our destination, howsoever late it was.

It was after about an hour of crossing a small town called *Jhumri Talaiya* that the incident of an ambush by the villagers took place in a densely populated village.

❧ ❧ ❧

Realising that we were under an act of sudden aggression, we reacted by pointing our loaded weapons towards the attackers. I shouted loudly in Hindi, "Stop, we are from the Indian Army."

By now, the attackers had come closer to us. On hearing me and seeing us all in military battle dress, their leader raised both his arms and called out, 'Military!' and all of them immediately halted, stepped back and lowered their weapons.

The leader of the attacking group was a middle-aged man who cautiously came up to me and said in broken Hindi, "Sorry for all this. We are guarding the village against the dacoits, who often come at night and rob the villagers of their belongings, mainly the cattle. So, every night, 20 adults of the village stay awake and guard the village to shoo the dacoits away if they try to enter."

Their leaders once again apologised for trying to attack us by mistaking us for dacoits. On my enquiring whether they had asked the local police to take action against the 'dacoits', the leader informed that they had informed the police several times but to no avail.

He further told me that the nearest police station, which was about 70 kilometres away, had just about 10 policemen and the SHO had expressed his inability to provide any protection to the villagers. Moreover, there were no means of telecommunication, and even the roads were not good enough to get any bus service operational. So, they were left to fend for themselves.

For me, the entire situation seemed very strange. Coming from a peaceful state like Himachal Pradesh where law and order was not an issue at all, it was difficult for me to imagine such a hopeless situation for the citizens.

Yet Another Shocker

After about an hour of moving ahead on our route, we came across a bullock cart approaching from the opposite direction. Four men carrying sticks were also walking along. There was some load in a large jute sack kept on the cart. Surprisingly, only one person was sitting in front who was guiding the bullocks. It was a bit odd, as generally, people travelling long distances would sit on the cart, particularly at night.

We enquired who they were and where they were headed. One of them, who could speak Hindi, replied that a person in their village was murdered and cut into pieces early morning on the previous day. One of the villagers had gone on foot to the police station, which was about 40 kilometres from their village. But the SHO asked him to bring the dead body to the police station for investigation and post-mortem, as the investigating officer (IO) was busy and could not spare 2-3 days to go to their village, investigate the murder, and come back.

They then decided to carry the pieces of the body in a sack to the police station for investigations. I wondered that after decades of independence, what kind of police administration it was! I also pondered how the investigating officer (IO) would carry out a fair investigation of the murder without visiting the scene of the crime. Apparently, human life hardly seemed to have any value, as the IO was busy with other 'more important things'.

We reached Kashipore village at about 0200 hrs. The village was about 4 kilometres short of enemy defences. Though a big village, the layout of Kashipore offered a surprising look. The houses made of mud with thatched roofs were situated in 5 different clusters, with all clusters about 300 to 400 metres apart. The explanation for this strange layout was revealed to me a little while later.

Worn-out after a long walk, we were virtually starving and required something nutritious to eat before sleeping. With a view to getting shelter for rest and some nourishing food, we knocked on the door of one of the houses in the cluster nearest to us.

After a while, a weary man half-opened the door. I informed him in Hindi that we were from the Indian Army and wanted a room for the night. But the blank look on the face of the man indicated that he did not understand a word of what I said. We tried again in English but to no avail. He then pointed in the opposite direction towards another bunch of houses and uttered something in Bengali. What we could make out was that Muslims in the other cluster understood Hindi (or Urdu?) and that we should go to them.

We then moved in the opposite direction, towards the group of houses suggested by the man, and knocked at the door of one of the bigger houses there. After a few knocks, a bearded middle-aged man opened the door. He hesitated a bit on seeing the uniformed personnel at that hour. I told him in Hindi that we were from the Indian Army and wanted a room to stay for the night and, if possible, a couple of cockerels on a payment basis.

He was kind enough to open a vacant small room for us, with an indigenous *Chulha* (fireplace for cooking) in it, with some fuel-wood stacked in one corner. His name was Latif. He spoke Urdu and could converse with us in Hindi.

While we were unpacking, Latif brought two live chickens and a large aluminium utensil for cooking. I paid him the cost of the fowls, which he reluctantly accepted. Hurriedly, rice and chicken were cooked, which we all ate hungrily.

The following morning, while interacting with villagers, we came to know that the groups of houses were segregated on the basis of caste and religion. Within the same village, the first group of houses was exclusively that of Brahmins, while in the other direction were the houses of Rajputs. Similarly, the houses of Bhumihars, the underprivileged sections, and Muslims were in different directions and exclusive clusters.

More surprising was the fact that within the village, the communication between the two groups was at a bare minimum. Even the places of worship and water sources were maintained separately by the inhabitants of some of the clusters. It pained me to see the caste and religion so deeply entrenched in rural India, something I could not imagine living in a town of Himachal Pradesh during the earlier days of my life.

Before leaving for the recce, we organised ourselves into three sub-groups. The sub-group led by me was to gather intelligence about the location of the enemy battalion HQs with its grid references, the location of the telephone exchange, and the deployment of Mortars and Medium Machine Guns (MMGs), if any. The other two sub-groups were to gather information about the defence deployment pattern, the location of three enemy platoons, and anti-tank recoilless (RCL) guns, if any.

We had the whole day and the next night to gather the information before catching up with the battalion. To camouflage our Army identity, we decided to wear worn-out vests, *dhotis*, and *pagaries* (cloth headgear) which we borrowed from the locals by paying them.

We decided to walk barefoot after keeping our bags in the room provided by Latif. There were a lot of villagers loitering around the defences, perhaps to see what the Army personnel were doing. To avoid the attention of the 'enemy' troops, we mingled with the local people.

That enabled all three sub-groups to easily walk through the enemy defences and gather information about the strength and deployment of the 'enemy'. There were some areas in the defences that were not accessible to the civilians. Information about such areas was collected by using a pair of binoculars from some vantage points in the vicinity.

Attack operations during the exercises were mock in nature, but the defences were actually prepared by digging up the trenches. The support weapons were also deployed strategically. Every part of the exercise was supervised by a few officers nominated as neutral umpires. All operations during the exercise, including the protection of the defences and the conduct of the raid, were observed and assessed by the umpires.

The enemy defences were spread over 3 to 4 square kilometres on a low-rise plateau. After surveying their deployment, we plotted their location details on the map to work out the grid references. The same exercise was done for the location of their battalion support weapons like mortars, MMGs, and RCL guns.

My sub-group had to do some additional walking, as the battalion HQ's location was about two kilometres behind the main defences. The entry of civilians to that area was blocked by the 'enemy'. Two of us climbed up a big tree close by and used our binoculars to get the exact location and deployment of troops & weapons around it.

I made a mental note of many other things like the layout of field telephone lines, the location and number of sentries and the total number of personnel manning the mortars, MMGs and RCL guns etc. That was important to me, as those details would be handy while executing the second task of raiding the enemy HQs.

By the last light, all three sub-groups met at a designated place before moving back to our base at Kashipore village. I compiled the gathered information and passed it on to the battalion HQ over the radio set to enable the CO to fine-tune his preparations for the attack. The CO also directed me to join the main columns of the battalion the next day before 1400 hrs.

Next early morning, we quickly walked around the enemy areas once again and looked for some additional information or changes before falling back to Kashipore. My patrol joined the battalion as per the given timeline and, along with other officers, attended the verbal orders of the CO for the task. I was glad that a lot of information provided by me was used in planning the conduct of the operation. The time of the attack (H-hour) was 2200 hrs.

The Brigade Commander, who was present during the verbal orders, was apparently happy with the preparations. In his briefing, the CO informed him that half an hour before the H-Hour, I would raid the enemy battalion HQs. In addition to disrupting their command and communication channels, my team was also made responsible for destroying a few battalion support weapons as well.

At 1630 hrs, I gave out the detailed verbal orders for the raid operation in the presence of the Brigadier and my CO. The Brigade Commander had a few questions to which I could reply to his satisfaction. After a light dinner, we left the battalion area at around 1900 hrs and began our movement stealthily towards the enemy defences. Later, my battalion was to move towards the assembly area at 2100 hrs and wait there for a success signal from me before moving to the FUP (forming up place) to launch the attack as planned.

Since my team was well-versed with the topography and deployment of the 'enemy' defences, we swiftly entered the area from the rear by maintaining complete surprise. Before executing the raid, we split into two groups. The first group snapped the telephone lines of the 'enemy' and symbolically destroyed their telephone exchange using mock explosives.

At the same time, the group led by me first raided the support weapon area and 'destroyed' a few mortars and RCL guns. Both the teams then swiftly invaded and 'destroyed' the control room of their battalion HQ with an array of hand grenades, rifle grenade launchers and dummy explosives.

A complete surprise maintained by us before the raid did not give the enemy any reaction time to effectively interfere with our action. While retreating, one of my men was 'captured' by a pursuing team of the 'enemy'. Notwithstanding that part, the raid was termed as "successful" by the umpire accompanying us.

At that point in time, using my very light pistol, I fired the success signal to indicate to my CO that the raid was successful. We then started our withdrawal to a designated position. Soon thereafter, we could hear the war cry of the Dogras, denoting that the attack was launched by my unit.

About an hour later, the exercise was called off by the GOC. We rushed back to a given RV to join the battalion there. At 0900 hrs the next morning, debriefing by the Brigade Commander took place. During the debriefing, all the operations were analysed threadbare, and the lessons learned during the exercise were clearly spelled out. The Brigade Major was asked to document the entire debriefing and share a copy with all the participating units. After the debriefing ended, the entire battalion moved back to its permanent location.

It was an exhilarating experience to get the feel of a war-like situation. The most important lesson was that for success in any task, meticulous planning and preparations were as important as flawless execution. Later, throughout my professional career, this teaching served me very well and proved its veracity several times.

Debriefing is an integral part of all Army exercises and is considered as important as the initial briefing. The shortcomings in planning and preparations of such operations are pointed out by the senior-most officer, and the lessons learned for the future are explained. Not only this, the entire debriefing is documented by the staff officers at the formation HQs for future references. The aim is to ensure that the shortcomings, if any, are not repeated in future operations.

The healthy practice of debriefing is virtually non-existent outside the Army. More mistakes mean more lessons learned for the future. Later in my professional career, wherever I worked, I ensured to schedule a debriefing session for my team after every important event that the team handled.

Chapter IX

Life At High-Altitude Border Area

"We live by chance, we love by choice and we kill by profession."

–A quote prominently displayed
at the firing range in OTS.

Freezing snow all around during the early morning hours of November seemed meaningless, as we all were sweating profusely. Sepoy Daleep Singh climbing the icy cliff ahead of me slipped on a thick layer of the hardened snow and skidded back by a few yards, pushing me also down the slope. That's when I once again assumed the lead.

It was quite tricky to climb up during the early morning hours under a clear sky when the ground snow on the foot-track had virtually turned into ice. There was still about an hour of stiff climb left before we expected to reach a flatter plateau. Before we encountered the vertical climb about an hour ago, we were already fatigued after walking more than 14 kilometres in snow.

It was extremely laborious and dicey to go from Natkusu post to Bazdan under the given conditions. The snow clothing itself was quite heavy, and the weight of the service weapon and the ammunition made the climb more ticklish. Even the snow boots couldn't help us stay balanced.

As we gradually inched upwards, the snow cover became thicker, and the intensity and velocity of cold winds increased. The north-eastern face of the mountain ensured that the temperature remained several notches below zero degrees Celsius, even after we were greeted by the first rays of the rising sun. To protect our eyes from the glitter of bright sunlight, we immediately put on our snow goggles, lest we suffered snow blindness.

After another hour of tricky and hard climb from Natkusu post upwards, the climb became suddenly gradual and walking up on the plateau made the going a bit easier. The sunshine from that point onwards seemed warmer, as the wind velocity suddenly decreased considerably.

We had gained quite a bit of altitude, and I could sense the lack of oxygen in the air, but not enough to cause any serious discomfort in breathing. After walking up the gradual incline for two more hours, we could see Bazdan Pass in the distance. The round and bald peak, under a thick cover of snow, sparkling in bright sunshine, looked like an inverted silver pot.

A couple of days ago, I received a telegram from my brother, informing me about the demise of my grandmother.

I wanted to be with my bereaved family during the mourning days. Upon my request, I was granted 10 days of casual leave.

Two heavy snowfalls had already taken place in the area, and Bazdan Pass as well as the entire road from Ranzalwan to Dandipore were closed for vehicular traffic. Anyone going out or moving into the area was required to walk the distance between Ranzalwan and Dandipore base by crossing Bazdan Pass.

I, along with 10 soldiers who were also proceeding on leave, left the battalion area at about 0230 hrs on the morning of 1ˢᵗ November. Early morning departure was mandatory, firstly because the entire distance needed to be covered before the last light of the next day. Secondly, and more importantly, the route up to Natkusu was highly avalanche-prone. This was the primary reason for the early morning departure, as daytime movement was prohibited there.

When we started our journey from Ranzalwan that morning, the temperature was around minus 6 degrees Celsius. Right from the word go, it was an arduous walk over the icy track. The progress was obviously slow, but a track was already made by the leave detachments regularly moving up and down.

We were equipped with proper winter dress including snow socks and boots, coat parkas, warm inners, balaclava woollen caps, snow goggles, etc. This made our movement easier for the first phase of our journey till Natkusu.

Earlier, it had taken us about 4 hours to cover a distance up to Natkusu post. A simple Aloo-Puri breakfast with a hot cup of tea seemed more than welcome there. Re-energised after breakfast and some rest, we were prepared to negotiate a steeper ascent towards Bazdan when we left at around 0745 hrs.

⋟ ⋟ ⋟

Minutes before noon, we reached Bazdan and had lunch there. The snow-covered peaks in the distance, glimmering under bright sunshine, offered a splendid view. Strong winds at the pass, however, made it quite challenging to stay outdoors. The JCO in charge of the Bazdan post told us that the afternoons during winter were generally breezy and cold there.

After a filling lunch, we resumed our journey. From there onwards, it was all going downhill up to Dandipore. To start with, moving down the gradual descent seemed easier. But after a while, as soon as the slopes became steeper, it seemed as enduring as climbing up.

After about two hours of careful descent, we approached Zagbal post and had a hot and energising cup of tea there. By then, the long hours of walking on snowy tracks in mountainous terrain started to reflect on our stamina.

Going downwards from Zagbal to Dandipore took us around two hours. As we moved down the hill, the snow cover receded, making things relatively easier. When we were about four kilometres short of our destination for the day, the snow disappeared. At that point, we were relieved to find a one-tonne Army truck waiting for us on the road.

The truck was sent there to pick us up by the officer in charge at Dandipore base. It was already dark when we reached our base camp and spent the night in the comforting 'warmth' of the Kashmir valley.

I left Dandipore very early the next morning to reach the transit camp Srinagar, from where I booked a current seat for myself on the officers' bus leaving for Jammu after about an hour. I reached Jammu Transit camp at 1800 hrs after a quick lunch break at Udhampur camp on the way. By 2030 hrs, I was on a night bus bound for my native place.

I spent a few days at Bilaspur with my parents and family and was fortunate to be there for the *Rasam Kirya* ritual. Upon completion of the leave period, I returned to Jammu by a night bus. An Army bus took me to Srinagar Transit Camp the same day. A battalion driver with a vehicle was waiting there to take me to Dandipura.

The next day, early in the morning, I began the ascent from Dandipura to Bazdan with a group of a few more boys from the unit returning from leave. This time, the journey to Ranzalwan via Bazdan Pass did not seem that taxing. I crossed Bazdan

Pass on foot for the second time within a few days. As per the standing orders, the entire group was required to wait at Natkusu until midnight to resume our travel through the avalanche-prone gorge. We left Natkusu post at around 0200 hrs and reached Ranzalwal early the next morning.

Winters at Ranzalwan

At Ranzalwan, it was routine as usual. One more spell of snowfall had taken place during my leave, and everyone was geared up for a long and severe winter ahead. Before the end of November, three more snowfalls took place.

Though belonging to a warmer place in Himachal, I had spent three years at the University campus in Shimla, experiencing three winters with snowfall there. But the high intensity and massive quantity of snowfall at Ranzalwan was something I could hardly have imagined.

The snow generally fell in very heavy flakes and within a couple of hours, two to three feet of snow would accumulate. The month of November itself was very cold, making the nights a bit uncomfortable even with the warmth of a sleeping bag and a Kerosene *Bukhari* warming up the underground bunkers all the time.

Once a week, every young officer was deputed to be on night duty and was supposed to be in the office the whole night. Night duty also involved checking the guards and sentries a few times at night for their alertness. Moving out in sub-zero temperatures with several feet of standing snow for sentry checking was a tough job, and I always wondered how tough it had been for the soldiers who performed sentry duties in the freezing nights for two hours at a stretch.

Day routine during the winter would begin with PT in the morning, which consisted of jogging for about 40 minutes with snow boots and other winter clothing on. There was not much paperwork in the office during the day, as limited Dak would come from Dandipura, that too once a week in a helicopter.

The weekly chopper sortie would also fetch some fresh vegetables, fruits, and bread. But on some of the scheduled days, the chopper flight would be cancelled due to bad weather. For the helicopter to land and take-off, the soft snow on the helipad was required to be beaten before every landing, particularly after every fresh snowfall.

A novel way was devised to keep the snow beaten all the time on the helipad. To beat the snow on the hockey ground used as a helipad, rugby matches between officers and the troops were played there every day. Colonel Mehra and Major DS Behuria would also make it a point not to miss any game. Playing most of the other outdoor sports, however, was not possible in the snow.

One half-hour game of rugby would leave all of us dead tired. It was great fun, as it strengthened the bond of the officers with the troops on the one hand and also kept the fresh snow beaten for easy landing and take-off of the chopper, on the other. Most of us would look forward to playing rugby every day. Even when it was snowing, the game was not missed, as it was even more fun playing on softer snow.

Ranzalwan was in close proximity to the LoC, but there were no hostilities. Our spare time between the lunch break and rugby games during the day was generally spent in the officers' mess playing Bridge or Rummy. After dinner, also, until about 2200 hrs, a few hands of Bridge and Rummy would invariably be played. Other indoor and board games like Carom, Chess, and Ludo were also available.

For entertainment of the troops at the battalion HQs, the CO had acquired a VCR along with an overhead projector (both gadgets had to be imported in those days) out of the battalion funds. A few video cassettes would be sent by the officer in charge at Dandipore by chopper every week, and a new Hindi movie would be screened inside a multipurpose hall for all ranks every Sunday evening.

An English movie was also screened for the officers and JCOs on Saturday evenings. The arrangement was truly a luxury in those days, as even the newspapers would reach us only once a week in a bundle, and that too if the helicopter sortie materialised. Surrounded by high mountains all around, there was no TV or radio reception at Ranzalwan.

A few black & white battery-operated TV sets were available at all the forward posts. The posts could catch the signal from Srinagar Doordarshan only after nightfall. Having a TV at such remote locations was an opulence in the year 1982 even though only *Doordarshan* channels were available for viewing. One large battery would last 5 to 6 days for 2 hours of TV viewing daily.

After it was discharged, the battery was brought on a mule's back to the battalion HQ for recharging. One extra charged battery was kept as a spare at every post.

Army Commander's Visit

At the end of February '83, we received a message regarding the visit of Lieutenant General K. Sunderji, the then General Officer Commanding-in-Chief (GOC-in-C) Northern Command (also referred to as Army Commander, Northern Army), to our unit. An outstanding officer who was originally commissioned in the Mahar Regiment of the Infantry, General Sunderji was the last former British Indian Army officer to go on to head the Indian Army from 1986 to 1988. As per the information received, he was to visit the general area Hurez for a few days. During his sojourn, the general was scheduled to halt at our unit HQ for one night.

The visit of an Army Commander is a rare event for any battalion. The unit carried out detailed planning, and everyone contributed to elaborate preparations for the visit. Specific responsibilities were assigned to all officers. A few days before the visit, we had to play a lot of rugby on snow to ensure that the snow on the helipad remained well beaten for smooth landing and take-off by the VIP helicopters. A day before the visit, we were fully geared up to welcome the Army Commander.

At around 1130 hrs on the designated day, two Indian Air Force helicopters landed at our helipad. It was a bright, sunny day. The place looked beautiful, with a thick snow cover glittering all around. General Sunderji, accompanied by his teenage daughter, Brigadier TS Rawat, the Brigade Commander, and a couple of staff officers, was warmly welcomed by all ten officers and 14 JCOS present at the HQ that day.

Sunderji was appeared to be a flamboyant, energetic, and young-looking Army general. He went around the HQS, the company lines, and the offices. Later, he met with all the officers in the sand model room, where the CO made an elaborate presentation on the battalion's operational preparedness.

In his honour, a lunch was organised as Bara Khana in the multipurpose hall, which was attended by all ranks present. General Sunderji interacted freely with the JCOs and *Jawans* during lunch. After learning about our modus operandi to beat the snow at the helipad, he wanted to play a rugby game with the officers and the troops that afternoon.

The rugby game with the Army Commander as one of the players was an event to remember for a lifetime. The general was very agile and nimble-footed on the field. He thoroughly enjoyed playing with the troops and interacted with many of them over a cup of tea after about 40 minutes of spirited play.

In the evening, a dinner was organised in the officers' mess. All the officers gathered there at 19:00 hrs. It was freezing outside, but the mess was kept warm with a few kerosene *bukharis* burning. The CO and all officers received the guest of honour at 19:30 hrs.

As the drinks were served, the younger officers got busy in a separate group, entertaining the general's teenage daughter with interesting anecdotes. In another corner of the mess, the seniors were busy having some serious discussions with the Army Commander and his staff officers.

When most of the young officers were busy chatting, I saw unit 2IC Major Behuria rushing towards the youngsters' corner. He came to me, pulled me aside and said, 'Shekhar, the Army Commander has expressed desire to see the officer who rescued 12 BSF men.'

He seemed quite excited. Holding my hand and virtually pulling me in the other direction, he said, 'Come on... come with me'.

The development was so sudden and unexpected that it surprised me. I followed the 2IC to the cosy corner where the GOC-in-C sat with Colonel Mehra and other senior officers. The CO introduced me to General Sunderji, who got up from his chair and gave me a warm handshake. Holding my hand tightly for a while, he said with a charming smile, "Well done, my boy. I am glad that you saved all my 12 men."

"Thank you, sir," I replied respectfully, "but it wouldn't have been possible without highly motivated boys of my team and the RMO. They all played an equally important role."

The GOC-in-C smiled with a nod.. Turning to Colonel Mehra, he asked, "JB, have you recommended him for a gallantry award?"

"Not yet, sir," Colonel Mehra replied with a bit of a fumble.

"Then what are you waiting for? He has saved 12 of my *Jawans*. Do it immediately," he directed.

The general then turned to Brigadier Rawat and continued, "TS, you coordinate and ensure that you carry the citation by hand tomorrow when we leave."

"Sure, sir," Brigadier Rawat gestured in the affirmative.

Colonel Mehra called for Dr (Captain) Walia and introduced him to General Sunderji. Sunderji shook hands with him as well and expressed his appreciation.

After meeting both of us, General Sunderji expressed his desire to meet the JCO and all the *Jawans* also who were part of the rescue patrol. Colonel Mehra assured him that all would be available at the helipad the next morning at the time of his departure.

The next morning, Subedar Deep Ram and all the soldiers who were part of the rescue team were made to fall in before the GOC-in-C arrived at the helipad. On his arrival, the general went straight to them. The CO introduced them to the Army Commander, who shook hands with all of them. He said a few words of encouragement to them before thanking the CO for the hospitality extended to him.

After the departure of General Sunderji, the CO thanked all the officers for working hard to make the visit successful. Later, during the day, I was told by Major Behuria that almost the whole of the intervening night, Colonel Mehra remained in his office to prepare a few citations for the gallantry awards. He further informed me that after breakfast, Colonel Mehra had handed over all the citations to Brigadier Rawat before submitting a compliance report to the general.

Chapter X

A Honey Trap?

"Keep your eyes and ears open, and your mouth shut"

–Samual Palmer

I could feel the sweat on my forehead. Was she really a health visitor, or had she entered the transit camp as a guest of an officer with a fake identity to trap someone like me? If that were the case, Captain Sharma's role was also doubtful. The turn of events that evening tended to support my suspicion.

My mind was working quickly. Maybe all I thought was not true, but I decided to be guarded rather than be sorry later. Thankfully, during the discussions so far, I was discreet enough not to disclose any information like my unit name, its exact current location, or any other important information that I was privy to.

As her next move, Deepa will perhaps try to extract some information after trapping me..

❧ ❧ ❧

Towards the end of September 1983, I received my posting orders as Training Company Commander in the Dogra Regimental Centre (DRC), Faizabad. I was called back from Ashok post days before my scheduled departure. Proceeding to join my new posting at the DRC involved crossing Bazdan Pass yet again, thankfully by road this time, as the pass was still open for vehicular traffic.

A few days before my posting orders arrived, a notification was issued by the Army HQs, requiring the SS-28 course officers to exercise their option either for a permanent commission in the Army or to leave the Army as a non-optee. The option was to be exercised before 15th February 1984. Knowing that the unit officers would not easily allow me to exercise the option to leave the Army, I decided to do so only after joining the DRC.

On the eve of my departure, as per the traditions of the armed forces, the battalion officers organised a farewell dinner for me. The choicest of scotches flowed. But for obvious reasons, the menu primarily comprised tinned stuff, except for chicken procured locally and fish from the river flowing close by. A mutton dish was also there, as some live sheep were available as 'meat on hoof' supplied by the Army Services Corps. Speeches with lavish praise from a few officers and the CO flattered me generously. The party concluded with my speech thanking all of them, and, finally, a memento was presented to me by the unit officers.

The next day, I reached the Dandipore base camp by lunchtime but could not leave for Srinagar due to the unavailability of a vehicle. For my onward journey, I had taken a day off in Srinagar to do some sightseeing.

On the following morning, I left Dandipore at around 0600 hrs in an Army Jonga. Upon reaching the transit camp at Srinagar, I had a hearty breakfast and changed into civilian clothes to explore the beautiful city.

I thoroughly enjoyed the outing, as it was the first time I did so in Srinagar. It was an experience of a lifetime going around the spectacular and iconic places like Dal Lake, Char Chinar, Chashme Shahi, Shalimar Bagh, Nishat Garden, and Shankaracharya Temple. After a memorable day, I returned to the transit camp at around five in the evening.

I rested for a while in my room and called for a cup of tea. Unlike the comfortable daytime temperature, the evening had suddenly turned cold. Wearing a parka coat, I went to the officers' mess early, around 1900 hrs. To keep myself warm, I thought of having a drink and headed straight to the bar. There were five other officers sitting near the bar, one of them with his wife.

I looked around for any acquaintances but could not find anyone. Sitting on a bar stool, I asked the barman for a drink. My drink was being prepared when I heard clacking sounds made by the high heels of a lady's stiletto shoes. I turned towards the sound and found a young lady entering the bar room with her male companion. They occupied a table next to the bar counter, very close to my seat.

I suddenly felt an intriguing stare from the young couple. While talking to each other, they were looking at me with a friendly smile. I tried to place them but could not, as neither of the faces looked familiar. *'Are they discussing me?'* I wondered.

Without looking directly at them, I threw a few glances at them. The man, presumably an army officer, seemed to be around thirty, with a medium height and a slim build. What surprised me was his turnout. His oversized formal jacket and its mismatched colour combination with his loosely fitting trousers gave him a shabby look. Shockingly, he was wearing a pair of flip-flops on his feet, which was like a cardinal sin inside an Army mess.

In contrast, the lady was fairly tall, and with her fair complexion and poise, she looked quite elegant. Around 25 years of age, she had neatly tied up her hair in a round bun on top of her head. She wore dark brown trousers, a light-coloured shirt, and a smart-fit beige jacket. A small red *bindiya* on her forehead indicated that she was married.

Sipping my drink and unable to curb my human instinct, I threw another covert glance at them. Still, I had to take my eyes off immediately because now the officer was virtually pointing at me. *Have I met them earlier?* I was still not sure.

I then noticed the gentleman approaching the bar. He occupied a vacant stool next to me. Posing as oblivious to his presence, I kept sipping my drink. After a while, I felt a soft pat on my shoulder.

As I turned to him, he offered his hand, saying, "Hello, I am Captain Sharma from the Artillery," naming some Medium Regiment of the Artillery, which I could not catch.

"I am Captain Shekhar from the infantry," I said as I shook his hand. We then exchanged pleasantries. Captain Sharma ordered a large double for himself and a small dry gin with lime cordial for the lady.

While the drinks were being prepared, Captain Sharma informed that his regiment was on Srinagar's outskirts. He then told me that he had returned from his annual leave and would proceed to his unit's location the next morning.

As soon as the barman prepared his drinks, Sharma excused himself and carried the drinks to his table. Handing the glass of gin to the lady, he sat down and took a few sips. Once again, I felt that they were discussing me.

Within a few minutes, Captain Sharma got up with his drink in his hand, walked up to the bar again, and occupied a stool beside me. Dragging his stool closer to me, he whispered, "I am sure you are a bachelor. Aren't you?"

Without waiting for my reply, he looked at me with a raised eyebrow. And then, with a cunning smile, he said, "Do you want to have a good time?"

I was dumbstruck by the implication of what he said. Such bizarre behaviour was unheard of in the Army. I was yet to recover from the initial jolt when I heard him say, "Come along, I'll introduce you to Deepa." Then he virtually pulled me by my hand towards his table.

I looked at him scornfully. *What an ignoble man!* I found myself in a completely alien situation. My heart began to beat rapidly as we reached his table. I was waiting to see how low a man could stoop.

Captain Sharma introduced me to her, "Meet Captain Shekhar from the infantry, and she is Deepa."

Displaying the respect expected of an officer towards a lady wife, I wished her with folded hands. Nodding her head gently, she responded with a meaningful smile, which I could not decipher. She then offered me her hand for a handshake. Hesitatingly, I also extended my hand, which she shook with a firm grip. She continuously looked right into my eyes, which made me even more nervous.

"Excuse me," Captain Sharma said as he got up and walked up to the bar to recharge his glass after finishing his large double in a single gulp. Sitting alone at a table with another officer's wife not well known to me seemed quite awkward. I was still trying to overcome my nervousness when I saw Captain Sharma walking out of the bar with his drink and moving towards the TV room.

"Where is your unit located?" I heard the lady say. *She speaks like a typical Army lady*, I thought.

'We are on the LoC, Ma'am,' I replied respectfully, deliberately holding back the details about my unit's location.

"Are you proceeding on leave or coming back?" she further inquired, drawing her chair closer to me.

"You may say I am going on leave, Ma'am," I replied, remaining discreet about my new posting details.

"Please drop that 'Ma'am' thing. You look to be my age, so call me Deepa," she said with a broad smile. I was surprised to see the lady getting so informal. At the same time, I sensed her spoken English was a bit jerky with an accent.

We discussed general topics for a while. My discomfort increased as she tried to be friendlier. I repeatedly looked towards the TV room, hoping to see Captain Sharma returning to the table. While conversing with her, I maintained proper decorum as was expected of an officer when speaking to a lady, and persisted with the prefix 'Ma'am' while addressing her. In the meantime, she asked the waiter to repeat her drink.

Then suddenly, the lady shifted her chair precariously closer to me. Taken aback by her bold manoeuvre, I tried moving away from her but found my chair stuck against the wall. There was no room for me to shift further away.

"Srinagar is a very boring place," she almost whispered in my ear. People say it is heaven, but to me, it feels like heaven only when I am in the company of a man like you." She gazed at my face as she spoke.

Desperately wanting to escape the situation, I shifted my weight in the opposite direction. Gesturing towards the TV room, I got up and said, "I'll go and look for your husband."

"Listen, Shekhar," she almost shrieked and grabbed my hand.

Lowering her voice, she continued, "Are you thinking Captain Sharma is my husband? He is just a friend like you."

Oh God, they are not married.

'I am really very sorry, I wrongly presumed it, Deepa,' I said, pulling my chair to the other side of the table. While apologising to her, I dropped the prefix 'Ma'am' for the first time.

'Not an issue, I just wanted you to know,' she said with another bewitching smile.

'Whenever Captain Sharma is in Srinagar, we spend some good time together,' Deepa continued unabashedly. 'But of late, I have realised that he is more interested in drinks than I.'

Knowing that she was not a lady wife, I found myself a bit at ease now. But at the same time, the situation had turned rather intricate for me. With two drinks down her throat, she seemed to have shunned all her inhibitions.

"If you extend your stay here for one more day, tomorrow we can spend the whole day together," Deepa said. "I will also take a day off and take you around the city, watch a movie, have dinner together and of course, have a lot of fun." She paused momentarily, winked at me and continued, We will then stay in a hotel for the night. How do you find this idea?"

I was startled. I had come across a few freaky females in the past, but never in my life was I confronted with such an open and 'straightforward' talk by a lady.

'You can pick me up from the MNS hostel in the morning, which is very close to this transit camp.' Observing that I was listening attentively, she continued, 'Just wait for me outside the hostel gate, I shall meet you there at 10 AM sharp.'

"So, you are a military nursing officer?" I said, trying to divert the discussion away from the topic.

"No," she said. "I am a health visitor in the Army Medical Corps, currently posted at the Military Hospital here and staying in the hostel of the military nursing service officers' mess."

I wanted to cut short the discussion and said, "Let us discuss tomorrow's plan over the dinner table." We finished our drinks and left for the dining room. On the way, I saw Captain Sharma with two other officers, apparently boozing heavily. I went over to him and asked him to dinner. Without replying, he gestured to me to go ahead, wanting to have more drinks.

The dining room was not yet crowded, as most officers were still at the bar. While having dinner, Deepa talked most of the time. Now and then, she would give me intriguing looks with inviting smiles. But my mind was busy figuring out how to wriggle out of the intricate situation.

After finishing the meal, we were served dessert. By then, a few more people had come to the table for dinner. Deepa was quiet for a while, fearing that others at the table could overhear our conversation.

Then out of the blue, something struck me. I was no Casanova and did not have extraordinary looks. I was an average young officer of the Indian Army. It was baffling how an unknown young lady health visitor became so interested in me in the first meeting itself. The thought that sparked in my mind was, in fact, a question. *Was it a honey trap, like the one used in the famous Samba spying case of the late seventies?*

The Samba Spying Case was a Cold War military intelligence programme that eventually emerged as a scandal in the Western Command of the Indian Army a few years ago. Almost 50 Army personnel, including a Brigadier, a few Colonels, Majors, Captains, JCOs, and NCOs, all belonging to one brigade, were arrested by the intelligence agencies on the testimony of two Pakistani spies who were apprehended by the Army.

The accused Indian Army personnel involved in the scandal were charged with supplying some classified information and documents to enemy intelligence agencies. There was a *modus operandi* to honey trap the Army personnel. A few good-looking young ladies with fake identities were used to get friendly with the Army officials. Using spy cameras, the military personnel were videotaped in compromising positions with the ladies. The videos were then used as blackmail tools to extract classified information and documents from them.

Is Deepa also part of a similar network, and will I be the next victim?

❧ ❧ ❧

By the time I finished the dessert, I had decided what to do. She suggested we go out for a stroll on the lawns to firm up the plan for the following day.

We slowly walked out of the mess building. Cool, fresh air welcomed us outside, but my mind was still occupied. As we walked towards a darker corner of the lawn, Deepa tried to lean on me, but I moved my shoulder away. She then put her arm around my waist. Out in the cold, I could feel a few droplets of sweat dripping down my spine.

I softly nudged her aside and politely told her that we had the entire day ahead to ourselves. Confirming that I would stay back, I told her to meet me outside her hostel gate at 10 a.m. the next morning. She was delighted, but at the same time, she cautioned me not to enter the hostel, as no males were allowed there.

During our walk around the lawn for a few more minutes, we generally discussed the sightseeing plan for the next day. But all through, Deepa kept trying to get closer to me. Then it was time for her to leave, as she said that her hostel gate was to close at 2130 hrs. I saw her off outside the main gate of the transit camp and bid her goodnight. That was the last time I saw her.

Getting back to the transit camp, I went to the reception and informed the official in charge there to reschedule my departure the next morning. I requested a seat on the bus leaving for Jammu at 0730 hrs instead of the 0930 hrs bus I had booked earlier. A seat was available, and the change was put into effect.

The next morning, I boarded the Army bus leaving for Jammu. When I entered the bus, I felt relieved to escape a sticky situation. As I occupied the seat allotted to me, I noticed an officer of the rank of Major from the Dogra Regiment sitting next to me. I wished him and introduced myself.

"Glad to be seated with a regimental officer here. Which Battalion?" The Major asked me smilingly, as the bus began to move. I told him that I was from 27 Dogra.

"I am from 10 Dogra, currently on a posting in the Corps HQ located at Srinagar." While he spoke, I read the nameplate hooked on his shirt. His name was Major K. K. Tiwari. He informed me that he had put in about 14 years of service. During the first few minutes of interaction with him, I understood that he was a knowledgeable and brilliant Army officer.

Major Tiwari was aware of my unit's location. When discussing his job profile, he told me that one of his responsibilities included collecting and disseminating military intelligence by coordinating with the civil intelligence agencies and the Army Intelligence Corps.

The discussion with him during the travel seemed very informative. Before the bus reached Udhampur Transit Camp and halted there for lunch, we discussed several topics of general and military interest.

The halt at Udhampur lasted one hour. While having lunch, it occurred to me that I could discuss the previous evening's episode with Major Tiwari. After all, he was experienced and coordinated with the intelligence agencies. *Yes, no one will be better equipped than him.*

Bus travel from Udhampur to Jammu was almost a two-hour journey those days. As the journey resumed after lunch, I discussed the previous evening. Giving Major Tiwari a complete account of the incident, I shared my suspicion, clarifying that it was just a thought based on my observations without any substantial evidence.

Major Tiwari listened to me very carefully. After I finished my narration, he thought about it for a while.

"Your inkling may be right, Shekhar," Major Tiwari spoke in a low tone. "Whatever you experienced last evening is the replica of a typical honey-trap used by the enemy intelligence," he continued.

"Your suspicion gains credence from the fact that there is no post of a health visitor or health worker in the Army Medical Corps (AMC), and a young officer like you is not expected to know this fact."Tiwari seemed concerned as he spoke.

"Good that you shared all the details with me," he continued. "I will give the required inputs to the Army Intelligence Corps and ask them to investigate the matter. They will immediately start looking for Deepa or any other female in Srinagar who fits your description. The agencies will also be asked to keep an eye on all the guest visitors to the transit camps, in addition to taking other precautions."

Major Tiwari further mentioned that Captain Sharma would also need to be questioned. He then asked me for Captain Sharma's unit details. I told him that I didn't know much about him. Major Tiwari told me that he would get his particulars from the entry he made in the register of the transit camp.

On reaching Jammu, Tiwari bid me goodbye before retiring to his room, as he had a train to catch to his hometown in a couple of hours. I felt relieved on two counts—firstly, going by my instinct, I could successfully extract myself from a situation that could have created issues for me later. Second, and more importantly, the matter was incidentally brought to the attention of an appropriate officer.

I am not sure what finally happened in the matter, as I could not get a chance to meet Major Tiwari again.

Chapter-XI

Life at the Regimental Centre

"The safety, honour, and welfare of your country come first, always and every time. The honour, welfare, and comfort of the men you command come next. Your own ease, comfort, and safety come last, always and every time."

–Field Marshal Carriappa

My tenure at Ranzalwan left me with a bagful of wonderful memories. The experience I gained there over a period of one year remains part of my fondest memories of life. This is especially true because I decided to leave the Army after completing the initial contractual period of five years of short-service commission.

After joining the Regimental Centre, I found that the daily routine there was not very strict. Realising that there was a lot of free time in the evenings after the games, I resumed my preparations for the competitive examinations with renewed vigour, increasing the daily study time to 6-7 hours a day.

All the regimental centres of the infantry regiments are responsible for the training of newly recruited soldiers, also called recruits. In addition, various other non-operational responsibilities like record-keeping, regimental matters, newly raised battalions, regimental reunions, etc., are also assigned to the regimental centres.

As the training company commander, my responsibility was to impart proper training to all 120 recruits in my company and transform them from raw teenagers into combat-ready soldiers by the time they passed out to join the allocated battalions.

Training of the recruits would start with their PT in the morning, followed by marching drills, tactics, and weapon training classes during the day and a one-hour games period in the afternoon. Routine training was handled by the Training platoon commanders who were of the rank of *Subedar,* under the close supervision of the training company commander. I was, however, supposed to take personal care of a few important aspects of their training.

Most of the recruits were from a rural background. Also, being mostly teenagers, their exposure to life was limited. It required great care and caution to train them in the Army way.

During the first 2-3 weeks, the physical training seemed very tough to the recruits, which prompted some of them to request discharge from service. Instead of accepting such impulsive decisions, they were mentored with personal care and attention after identifying the reasons for such a hasty decision.

Civil Administration

While at the DRC, there were a few incidents worth recounting. One such incident was the process of getting a gun licence issued. The episode was not important because the license was important to me, but it was for the experience I got during the interface with the district administration at Faizabad.

In February 1984, Captain Sanjiv Sood, a colleague at the DRC, suggested that since I was leaving the Army, I should get a gun licence issued with all-India jurisdiction, as it would be relatively easier to get while in Army service. Captain Sood was also interested in obtaining one for himself.

Sood suggested that the Commandant could help us get the licences. So, both of us sought an appointment with the Commandant and personally requested that he speak to the District Magistrate (DM) for the issuance of gun licences. Brigadier Samba immediately agreed and spoke to the DM over the phone in our presence. After having spoken to him, the Commandant asked us to meet the DM in his office on the following day at 11.30 a.m.

The next morning, both of us went to meet the DM in his office. The visit left an everlasting impression on my young mind and gave me an insight into the functioning of civil administration in those days in a big state like Uttar Pradesh.

As we approached the district collectorate, I was surprised to see three-layer barricades and a tight security ring all around the office. A large number of people were lined up outside the barricades, waiting to be let in by the security personnel. Upon inquiring, it was revealed that barricading was a routine year-round arrangement.

The general public desirous of meeting any official in the DM's office was required to get their names and the purpose of the visit entered with the security personnel. One officer in the middle administration would then decide about the persons to be allowed to get in between 1500 hrs and 1530 hrs, after which the general public's entry was stopped.

Only the fortunate ones allowed entry into the barricades could meet the concerned officers. The rest of the public was denied entry for the day, only to try their luck on the following day again, if they so wanted.

Both of us were in Army uniform. We informed the security personnel at the entry point about our appointment with the DM at 1130 hrs. The officer in charge of security was very respectful and checked with the DM's Private Secretary (PS) on the intercom. It was only upon his confirmation that we were permitted to enter.

We were ushered into the visitors' room on reaching the DM's office. Six or seven people were already sitting there, and based on their attire, a few of them looked like politicians. The PS later toldus that there were two MLAs and one MP among them.

How the times have changed, I wonder now! That was the time when the top politicians of the district would wait for the DM in his office. But the tables have turned today. These days the political bosses have started summoning the DMs to their offices or houses!

The DM came to the office around noon and met with the MP and MLAs before we were called in. The office was in a large, lavishly furnished room. The DM, a middle-aged man, was dressed in a light grey safari suit.

The DM told his PS that we were there with a reference from Brigadier Samba and asked him to inform the Additional District Magistrate (ADM)-2 to issue an 'all India' gun licence each to both of us. As serving Army officers, police verification was dispensed with in our case. He specifically asked his PS to ensure the licences were issued on the same day.

The meeting with the DM lasted only for a few minutes. We came out with the PS, who then spoke to the ADM-2 over the intercom and sent one person to escort us to his cabin.

ADM -2 was an elderly person from UP State Civil Service who was very respectful while dealing with us. We handed him over the filled-in licence applications and all the required documents. He asked one of his attendants to deposit the arms licence fee for us, the amount of which was paid by us.

In the meantime, he offered us tea and spoke to us on a few topics of general interest. The ADM also expressed interest in knowing how the Army functioned. This was another time when I realised how limited the knowledge about the Army was even among well-placed persons in civilian life. After about an hour or so, he handed over the gun licences to us.

Faizabad is a fairly large district. We were told that there were 3 ADMs in the district, despite the fact that until then, no law and order problem related to the Ram Janam Bhumi-Babri Masjid conflict existed. We also learned that the DM had delegated most of his powers to the ADMs, and he would generally come late to the office and leave early by 1600 hrs.

Later in my career, after more than three decades when I visited Lucknow in 2017, I realised that the availability and approachability of senior civil servants in the State of UP had deteriorated further. As another retired officer from the same clan of civil services and working for the corporate sector, I experienced it when I tried meeting a couple of senior civil servants.

Getting an arms licence was my first exposure to civil administration. At that point, I was also aspiring to become a civil servant after quitting the Army. The visit to the DM's office prompted me to decide that if I made it to the civil services, I would remain approachable to the general public, irrespective of the state I was selected to serve.

We came out of the district collectorate happily, as the job was done quickly. But as we crossed the barricades, my heart went out to those still stuck at the entry gate, waiting to meet a district officer.

On reaching the DRC, we once again called on the Commandant and thanked him, informing that we had received the licences. He thanked the DM over the phone immediately. A few days later, both of us purchased double-barrel guns against our licences from a local arms dealer there.

Helping Sepoys Become Officers:

During the last few months of my tenure at the DRC, while preparing for the competitive examinations, I had the opportunity to assist two Sepoys in becoming commissioned officers. As per a prevalent scheme in those days, the opportunity was afforded to bright and meritorious soldiers with senior secondary qualifications to become commissioned officers in the Army.

Under the scheme, the candidates were required to pass an internal written examination. The successful candidates were then supposed to undergo the SSB interview for selection as trainee officers. I am told that a similar scheme exists even today.

All those who passed the SSB were required to undergo a three-year training course as cadets of the Army Cadet Corps (ACC) to graduate. The ACC graduates would then undergo military training for one year at IMA Dehradun to be commissioned as ACC Commissioned Officers in the Army.

The DRC made special arrangements to assist the regiment's promising young soldiers in qualifying for the SSB interviews. All the battalions were asked to send to the regimental centre all the *Sepoys* who qualified for the written test so that they could be imparted expert coaching for the interviews.

The soldiers generally join the Army as recruits at a relatively younger age by forgoing their chance to get higher education, which could have enabled them to become commissioned officers directly. The rationale behind the scheme, therefore, was to provide the bright young soldiers with another chance to be compensated for their missed opportunity.

That particular year, three *Sepoys* of the Dogra Regiment had passed the written examination for ACC commission and were called upon to undergo a coaching course at the DRC. Two out of the three, namely Yash Paul and Dev Raj, were from my battalion, while another *Sepoy*, Surat Ram, was from 26 Dogra.

I came to know about them in February 1984 when Yash Paul and Dev Raj came to meet me during the games period. They explained the reason for their visit to the DRC. Considering their respective ages at that time, that was the last chance for Yash Paul, while Dev Raj had two more chances.

Their SSB interviews were to be held in April. Yash Pal informed me that the coaching at the DRC was outsourced to an agency whose instructors were to start a 15-day capsule programme towards the middle of March. Until then, they were asked to prepare on their own.

I offered them that I could also provide them with some tips based on my personal experience with SSB, to which they gladly agreed. So I asked both of them to meet me after the sports period daily for about an hour for a daily session. The third candidate, *Sepoy* Surat Ram, also sought my permission to join in.

For the next six weeks or so, I coached them about every afternoon on various topics, including group planning, group tasks, leadership exercises, impromptu lectures, group discussions, psychological tests, thematic apperception tests, the Chairman's interview, tips to tackle the obstacle course, etc. In addition, I provided them with some finer tips to get an edge over the other candidates.

All three of them were very keen and receptive. I realised that because of their schooling in rural areas and limited exposure, their main handicap was oral communication in English, which required a major thrust within the given time frame. I devoted significant time to helping them improve their communication skills. Within weeks, all three of them made good progress and showed all-around improvement.

Even after their professional coaching programme began, I would take some time out in the evening to continue my sessions. Before they left for their respective battalions after about two months at the DRC, they seemed confident of qualifying.

Towards the end of May, a circular issued by the Commandant of the DRC mentioned that Yash Paul and Dev Raj were successful in the SSB interviews and were to join their ACC training by mid-June. Before they joined the training, both were called to the regimental centre again for a couple of days.

They met me once again and acknowledged that my inputs played an important role in their success. While it gave me immense satisfaction that two of them could make it, at the same time, I felt sorry for Surat Ram who had shown a lot of promise during the coaching sessions.

Later, in 1988, when I was working in the civil services and posted as SDO (Civil)-cum-SDM at Dehra in District Kangra (HP), Dev Raj met me. He hailed from a village near Dehra town. Dev Raj informed me that a few days ago, after completing his training at the IMA, he was commissioned as an officer in the Punjab Regiment, while Yash Paul was commissioned in theJat Regiment.

Another piece of information given by Dev Raj was that a year after his selection, Sepoy Surat Ram also made it to the ACC and was undergoing training at IMA Dehradun. Dev Raj later retired as a Lieutenant Colonel and remained in touch for many years.

Regimental Reunion

During my tenure at the DRC, I was fortunate to be a part of a regimental reunion. All infantry regiments generally celebrate their reunions every four years at their respective centres. During the reunion, many retired officers, JCOs and the other ranks (ORs) of the regiment can interact with their serving counterparts.

For the reunion at the DRC, the Commanding Officers and the Subedar Majors from all the battalions were invited. Several retired personnel of the regiment were also hosted as guests. All the retired soldiers of the regiment decorated with gallantry awards were given special invites. A ceremonial parade marked the occasion, in which four contingents took part.

I was among the four officers the regiment selected to lead the contingents. Lt General S S Sidhu, the 'Colonel of the Dogra Regiment', was the guest of honour. As per convention, a particular regiment's most senior serving officer is given the honorary status of Colonel of the Regiment.

General Sidhu took the salute of the parade and also presented the regimental colours to 32 Dogra, a newly raised battalion. The regimental colour is a regimental flag, especially designed for the newly created battalion, which is formally handed over to it during such reunions. The day of the colour presentation becomes a landmark day for any newly raised unit.

The reunion ceremony also had a *Bara Khana* for lunch, where all the officers, JCOs, NCOs, and recruits dined together, with the officers interacting freely with everyone. *Bara Khana* was followed by a grand regimental dinner at the officers' mess. Overall, the reunion ceremony was a resounding success.

My tenure at the regimental centre slightly differed from what I had done for four years while serving with my unit. As a training company commander, it was an exciting experience to train the newly recruited soldiers. In addition to my job experience, I gained a lot more diverse and valuable experience which enriched my professional and personal life in the following years.

Chapter-XII

The Republic Day Surprise

"I am a soldier, I fight where I am told, and I win where I fight."

–General George S. Patton, US Army

He seemed to be expecting my phone call as I heard him say, "Shekhar, can you come over to my house right away and have breakfast with us?"

"Sure, sir," I replied, still a bit confused by the last-minute invitation from the Deputy Commandant of the Centre. Before putting down the receiver on the cradle, I wanted to ask what the occasion was, but decided not to do so, as Colonel Sachdeva's house was next to the officers' mess. 'I would know the occasion on reaching there,' I thought. As per my wild guess, the occasion was perhaps the Republic Day.

'Maybe, he has invited all the young officers of the Regimental Centre to breakfast,' I told myself.

Four months earlier, I had joined the DRC at Faizabad. Since I was alone without family, I was allotted bachelor accommodation in the officers' mess, a spacious single room with a toilet. A few other young officers from various battalions of the regiment posted at the DRC, were also there in the mess, and I made good friends with many of them.

On my first day in office, I met Captain K C Chauhan, the Adjutant, who informed me that I had been assigned the responsibility of looking after No. 3 Training Company as the training company commander.

My dining in was a routine affair which started with drinks, followed by a rich menu for dinner, a few lectures welcoming me, and finally my address thanking everyone, The dining in marked my formal induction into the officer cadre there, after which I got going with my job.

Most senior officers posted at the Centre had an impeccable service record. I was particularly impressed by the working style of Colonel Sachdeva, who assumed most of the administrative responsibilities at the Centre and shouldered the maximum workload of the Centre Commandant. I was told that many improvements occurred during his tenure of the past two years at the DRC.

By November '83, the ongoing batch of recruits had completed their training and passed out after their Kasam Parade *as fully trained soldiers, allocated to various battalions of the Dogra Regiment. Soon after their passing out, a new batch of recruits arrived for training, and the same old routine began all over again. The only difference was that I was involved in their documentation for the new batch of recruits right from the beginning of their training.*

In the second week of January 1984, I exercised my option as a non-optee for a permanent commission. I could get an extended tenure of another five years, but I opted against it. In other words, I opted to leave the Army immediately after the completion of the initial contractual tenure of five years. After the higher-ups saw my option, the Deputy Commandant and the Commandant both asked me to meet them in their respective offices.

Both wanted to know why I had not opted for a permanent commission. I explained the rationale behind my decision to them. I also informed them about my ongoing preparations for the civil services examination and my wife's job. Having listened to me, both of them respected my decision, and the Commandant asked the Adjutant to process my option for onward submission to the Army HQ.

Had I been with the battalion while exercising the option, I was sure all the unit officers would have forced me to withdraw it and opt for a permanent commission. My posting away from the battalion made it easier for me to opt out of the Army.

It was the morning of 26th January 1984. After studying for a couple of hours , I was getting ready to go to the *mess for breakfast when, at about 0830 hrs, a **Jawan** in PT dress knocked at my door.*

After wishing me "Ram-Ram," he said that the Deputy Commandant had sent him to ask me to speak to him immediately over the phone. A little surprised by this unusual message, I hurried towards the mess and called Colonel Sachdeva using the intercom there.

❧ ❧ ❧

Minutes after receiving the telephonic invitation, I pressed the doorbell of Colonel Sachdeva's bungalow. He himself opened the door. He was meticulously dressed in formal clothes with a tidy maroon-coloured turban and neatly tied beard. Bearing the usual broad smile, he welcomed me while ushering me into his living room. I looked around for other invitees but couldn't see anyone. He offered me a seat on the sofa, which I hesitantly took. He also sat next to me.

Unexpectedly, Colonel Sachdeva got up from the sofa and once again offered his hand for a handshake to me and said, "Congratulations, Shekhar!"

Confused a bit, I also got up and shook his hand, still trying to figure out with a blank look. At least, it was clear to me that I was not being congratulated for the Republic Day,

"Last evening I received a logged wireless message from the station HQ, which I saw this morning," said the Colonel.

"We are informed," he continued, "that on this Republic Day, two officers from the Dogra Regiment have been conferred with gallantry awards by the President of India, and you are one of them." Colonel Sachdeva paused and gave me a hearty smile.

I held my breath as he further said, "For some gallant act that you might have done, you have been awarded a Sena Medal by the President of India."

It is a great honour for any Army officer to receive a gallantry award from the President. I was suddenly reminded of General Sunderji asking my CO to give citations by hand during his visit to our battalion HQ at Ranzalwan almost a year ago. *So, it was perhaps for the same rescue operation. Or was it for the raid that I conducted to capture Zunaid Khan?* I was not really sure.

Colonel Sachdeva then picked up a paper from his *Dak* pad, looked at it and said, "There are two more from your battalion who are in the Army Chief's awards category and have been conferred with the Chief of Army Staff's Commendation Card. They are Subedar Deep Ram and *Sepoy* Hem Raj."

I immediately knew that it was for the rescue mission. Personally speaking, I valued saving the lives of 12 fellow soldiers more than arresting a separatist. Moreover, the rescue mission was much more challenging and satisfying than the raid to capture Zunaid Khan.

"Now I know, sir," I said, "It was a rescue mission in which we extricated and saved 12 BSF *Jawans* trapped in heavy snow. It happened during the winters under adverse circumstances in a highly avalanche-prone area in North Kashmir."

Suddenly, I remembered Dr (Captain) Walia who had contributed immensely to making the rescue operation a success. "Do you have the complete list of Republic Day awards, Sir?" I asked Colonel Sachdeva .

"Yes, of course. Why do you ask?" he quizzed.

"Sir, has Dr (Captain) JS Walia from AMC been awarded something? He was then RMO with us and was instrumental in making the rescue operation a success," I replied.

"Okay, let me have a look at the list once again," replied the Deputy Commandant.

He then got up, went up to his study, and brought a bunch of papers. After flipping through the list for a while, he removed his spectacles and said, "Yes, I see his name there. He too has been awarded the Chief of Army Staff's Commendation Card."

That was the moment Mrs Sachdeva came to the living room. I got up and greeted the lady. She reciprocated and congratulated me warmly. She told me that they learned about my award early in the morning and decided to break the good news to me over breakfast.

Almost simultaneously, the landline phone rang, and the Deputy Commandant got busy on a call for a while. The lady excused herself to lay the table for breakfast. My thoughts again went back to the day when the mission was executed. I remembered the expression on the faces of Matadeen and his men when we located them under those horrid conditions.

"Breakfast is served," a call from Mrs Sachdeva interrupted my thoughts. By then, Colonel Sachdeva also got free from the call and invited me to the table. While having breakfast, the Deputy Commandant asked me to explain the details of the incident. I narrated the details of the entire rescue mission, which both of them listened to attentively.

After we finished breakfast and were chatting for a while at the table, Colonel Sachdeva remembered that I had exercised the option to leave the Army.

"I suggest you think over the option you exercised once again," he suggested. "I will ask the Adjutant to withhold it for a while, as we still have time to forward it to the Army HQ. The way you have performed in the Army, coupled with this medal, I am sure you will do very well in your career."

I wanted to say that my decision was final, but out of respect, I held my words back. Colonel Sachdeva picked up the phone, connected to the Adjutant, and asked him to withhold action on my option until further orders from him.

After spending another half an hour with them, I thanked the Deputy Commandant and Mrs Sachdeva for the wonderful breakfast and left.

"See you at the JCO's mess for Republic Day lunch," Colonel Sachdeva said.

I remembered that lunch was organised that day for all officers and JCOs at the JCOs' mess on the occasion of Republic Day.

"Sure, sir. Thanks again, and have a nice day," I said as I left his house.

I reached the officers' mess and found that almost all the young officers put up in the mess were standing on the lawns and enjoying the warmth of bright sunshine after breakfast. Everyone congratulated me, and while thanking them, I could guess that the Adjutant had broken the news to them.

At the designated time, all the officers and the JCOs assembled in the JCO's mess for lunch. Brigadier Samba congratulated me and then broke the news to all the officers and JCOs present. Some of the JCOs belonging to the other training companies, who were unfamiliar with me, introduced themselves to me. A few officers and JCOs wanted me to narrate the incident to them, which I briefly did.

Soon, a buffet lunch was served. While having meals, I noticed that the Commandant and the Deputy Commandant discussed something for a while, and then Colonel Sachdeva signalled me to come over. Brigadier Samba then told me there would be a formal dinner in the officers' mess that evening to celebrate the award of the Sena Medal to me. As I thanked him, the Deputy Commandant made a formal announcement to inform all the officers about the evening dinner.

In the evening, the officers began to gather in the mess after 1930 hrs. Though it was a routine formal dinner, the occasion was full of hospitable warmth. The Commandant also suggested to me to reconsider my decision to leave the Army. Without committing anything, I just nodded.

After dinner, the ritual of speeches began. The Commandant spoke a few good words in his formal speech. In my address, I thanked the Commandant and all other officers for the honour given to me.

The next day, I met the Deputy Commandant in his office and informed him that my decision to leave the Army was well-thought-out and was not taken because I did not foresee a promising career ahead. I then shared with him the details of my preparations to join the civil services and my family circumstances.

I further mentioned that the Army Rules permitted the non-optee SSC officers to pursue civil employment after exercising their options. I then requested him to forward the option already exercised by me to the Army HQ.

Colonel Sachdeva asked me a few questions before becoming convinced. He then checked the Commandant's availability over the intercom and took me to his office. I explained my point of view to the Commandant also and made the same request to him.

The Commandant specifically tried to drive home the point that every year, a large number of candidates appeared in the competitive examinations, but only a few finally made it. He wanted to know how sure I was about my success.

I respectfully informed him that there was no question of being too sure in the competitive examinations. However, I cited the incident of the interview call I received in the OTS after qualifying the State Civil Services examination, which had given me a lot of self-confidence.

I further told the Commandant that I had started my preparations several months ago and was fully prepared to appear in the ensuing examinations. The Commandant seemed to be convinced, picked up the intercom, and asked the Adjutant to process the option I exercised for submission to the Army HQ.

My application was processed and forwarded to the Army HQ in a couple of days. The decks were cleared for me to enter a new phase of life.

Back home, my wife Shashi was in the family way, and the expected time was the last week of March '84. I could get about two weeks off as casual leave to be with my wife at such a critical time, and I was fortunate that during my leave period itself, we were blessed with a lovely daughter, whom we named Kanika.

After I returned from casual leave, the advertisement for the civil services examination was out, and I submitted my application to the Union Public Service Commission. Soon thereafter, the State Civil Services (SCS) Examination was notified by the State Public Service Commission, and I applied there as well. The preliminary civil services exam was scheduled to be held on the first Sunday of June next, while the written examination for the State Civil Services was scheduled for the third week of August.

I needed to plan my leave as per the exam schedule. Accordingly, I met the Deputy Commandant and informed him about the dates. He suggested that I could proceed on 6 days' casual leave in June and then plan for 60 days of annual leave beginning 1st July onwards up to 29th August. On expiry of the annual leave, I was required to join the DRC on 30th August to be relieved on 1st September from Army service. That way, I could take the remaining papers of the civil services exam after getting relieved. The plan suited me well, and I applied for the leave accordingly.

The next two months seemed to have flown swiftly as I prepared for the preliminary examination, devoting 7 to 8 hours daily. I had already done some of the spadework during the past year, though much brushing up was still required.

6-day casual leave seemed to be over in a jiffy, with almost half of it gone in travel. But I was satisfied that I fared well in the prelims and hoped to qualify for the main examination. On rejoining my duties, I continued with my preparations. Since the syllabi for both the exams were almost similar, I had chosen the same optional subjects for both the examinations.

A few days after my return to the DRC, it was time for my two-month annual leave. I left after receiving good wishes from almost all the officers in the regimental centre. Back at home, I could devote 10 to 12 hours daily to prepare. With an infant to look after, along with her household responsibilities, Shashi unflinchingly supported me in my preparations, even despite her bank job. My mother looked after our daughter during my wife's office hours.

In July, the results of the prelims of the Civil Service examination were out, and I qualified for the main exams, expected to start towards the end of September. There were no prelims for State Civil Services in those days. Written examinations for the State Services exams commenced at the beginning of August and were over by the month end. I was quite satisfied with my performance and expected an interview call, though one could not be too sure in any all India exam where numerous candidates appeared.

As my annual leave ended, I left for Faizabad to join for a couple of days before saying farewell to arms. When I reached Faizabad on 29 August, one of my colleagues, Captain Avinash, told me that Colonel Sachdeva had made elaborate arrangements for my send-off.

On reaching my office the next morning, the Deputy Commandant summoned me. I went over to him, and he informed me that my farewell event would commence with a formal evening tea at the JCOs' mess on 31 August followed by a farewell dinner at the officers' mess. He also outlined the events planned for the morning of 1 September.

Listening to the complete details, I was pleasantly surprised to be treated the way it was planned. I asked Colonel Sachdeva whether I really deserved that kind of a grand send-off after putting in just five years of commissioned service.

The Deputy Commandant told me in no uncertain terms that, as a gallantry award winner of the regiment, I had more than earned the send-off he planned. I thanked him and also informed him about my passing the civil services preliminary examination and doing well in the State Civil Services examinations. He congratulated me and wished me success.

After office hours on 31st August and before I went to the JCOs' mess for my farewell tea party, Captain K C Chauhan, the Adjutant, informed me in confidence that the Deputy Commandant had been very firm right from the beginning that my send-off must be a grand affair. The Adjutant also told me that Colonel Sachdeva convinced the Commandant to agree, who initially was a bit reluctant and wanted it done routinely. However, the Commandant could not overlook Colonel Sachdeva's logic in treating me as an officer with 'distinguished service'.

Evening tea in the JCOs' mess went off well. Most of the JCOs seemed confused as to why I had decided to leave the Army at such a young age, without a pension or any other social security cover. Many thought the gallantry award was a good beginning for my bright future in the Army. A few of them wondered what I would do after leaving the Army.

After learning that I did not have any civilian job in my pocket, many seemed to wonder even more. The *Subedar* Major of the Centre suggested that with the decoration of the Sena Medal on my chest, I should have continued. I tried to justify my decision with my arguments, but most did not seem convinced.

The farewell dinner in the evening was a grand affair. After a couple of drinks, some of the officers got sentimental. A lavish dinner was served thereafter. After the dinner, the routine ritual of farewell addresses began. Four officers, including the Commandant and the Deputy Commandant, spoke some customary good words and wished me the best for the next phase of my life and career.

But the address by the Deputy Commandant stole the show and also made me emotional. Colonel Sachdeva used the choicest of words to appreciate me. I always had an inkling that Colonel Sachdeva had a special liking for me, and he made it more than obvious with his endearing speech.

At the end, it was my turn to thank everyone. As I stood up to speak, I realised that I was too young to deliver a 'word of thanks' in front of a crowd that mostly consisted of my seniors andelders. So, I decided to be very precise and brief in my address.

While describing the highlights of my Army career very briefly, I expressed my gratitude to all the officers for their cooperation and guidance during my one-year tenure at the Centre. I then sincerely mentioned that my short service in the Army would form an unforgettable part of the most valuable memories for the rest of my life. Towards the end, I outlined my plans to appear for the competitive examinations in a couple of sentences.

Once the ritual of speeches was over, the Commandant presented me a dinner set made of white metal with a silver coating on behalf of all the officers as a souvenir, on which the occasion and date were engraved, along with my name. I was then made to sit on an easy chair, which a few officers picked up in swinging motions, with a customary and loud chant of "he is a jolly good fellow".

I was carried to the portico of the mess, where an Army jeep was waiting. Before I sat on the jeep, hands were reciprocated from both sides. The jeep drove me to my room, which was just about 300 metres from the mess door in the same compound. Captain Jagdeep escorted me to my room.

The next day I got up early and while packing my limited baggage, I wondered about a conflict between the hierarchical structure and rich traditions of the Indian Army. When it came to welcoming and seeing off the officers, the seniority of the officer concerned did not seem to matter. In my case, the event was made a grand affair, much of which I had yet to witness that morning.

The day turned out to be a memorable one for me. After an elaborate breakfast at the Commandant's place, I was escorted by Captain Sanjiv Sood to the regimental temple where the religious teacher chanted some mantras and carried out a short *Puja* for a good future for me. From there, we went to the quarter guard, where the Adjutant and the Centre *Subedar* Major conducted me.

After the ceremonial guard saluted me, I recorded my comments in the inspection book. I was pleasantly surprised to find myself writing in an inspection book where only senior visiting officers had the privilege to do so. While writing my comments, I noticed that almost all the comments in the inspection book were written by officers of the rank of Brigadier and above, and I was perhaps the most junior to have the privilege of recording my comments in it.

A well-decorated open Willy jeep was waiting outside when I moved out of the quarter guard. It was the kind of jeep generally used by VIPs to inspect a ceremonial parade. I got into the jeep and stood holding a nickel-coated tee-rod affixed on its mounting space in the middle.

Two thick, long ropes were tied on both sides of the jeep's front bumper. All 16 officers present that day came forward to hold the rope on my right, led by the Deputy Commandant. The rope tied to the bumper on my left was held by all the JCOs, around 35 in number, led by the Centre *Subedar* Major.

Braving the hot and humid weather at the fagend of the monsoons, the officers and the JCOs in their smart turnouts began to pull the jeep, with a driver manning its controls. I suddenly realised that everyone pulling the jeep was older than me. It seemed a bit embarrassing to be pulled in an open jeep like that. But then, that was what the Army tradition warranted. They slowly pulled the jeep for a distance of about 500 metres from the quarter guard up to the main entrance gate of the regimental centre.

After crossing the main gate of the DRC, the jeep stopped, and I dismounted. The Centre Commandant was waiting there. I walked up to him and saluted. Brigadier Samba shook hands with me and wished me the best in the future. Another jeep and a one-tonne truck to carry my baggage to the railway station were already parked there.

Moved by the display of utmost affection and respect, I thanked and shook hands with all the officers and JCOs with moist eyes before embarking on the jeep meant to take me to the railway station. Five officers of the rank of Captain escorted me in another jeep. On reaching the station, I was pleasantly surprised to see Colonel Sachdeva also arriving there to see me off.

The DRC had hired a professional photographer to cover the event right up to my departure. Since there was still time for the train to arrive, some photography also took place at the station. The train arrived on time, and I had about ten minutes to board. Three Jawans were deputed to take care of my baggage; they helped me with all the loading and escorted me to my seat. Soon, the signal went down, and the train started moving. From my seat window, I kept waving at all the 'Dogras' present on the platform until the train picked up speed.

It was an extremely emotional moment. I knew that one phase of my life was over, only to pave the way for the next one. As per the regulations in those days, all the SSC officers who opted to leave the Army after 5 years were sanctioned 28 days' terminal leave beyond five years before they were finally released. On completion of the terminal leave, the officers were not required to join their duty station again before they were finally released.

While travelling back from Faizabad, I did not realise that my active association with the Army was still not over. A couple of notable incidents were still in the offing, which would make my brief Army career even more memorable.

After I reached home, I continued my preparations for the forthcoming examinations. I was still on Army rolls until my terminal leave ended on 29th September. A few days later, I received a telegraphic intimation from the Dogra Regimental Centre that an investiture ceremony for presenting the gallantry awards notified on the previous Republic Day was being held on 26th November in Mumbai. Investiture is a formal ceremony where officers who are to be awarded the gallantry awards are physically presented with the medals on behalf of the President of India.

In my case, I was to be presented with a Sena Medal by General AS Vaidya, the then Chief of Army Staff. General Vaidya had a very distinguished Army career. With some prestigious decorations to his credit, like Mahavir Chakra (MVC), Param Vishisht Seva Medal (PVSM), and Ati Vishisht Seva Medal (AVSM), he was among the most decorated officers of the Indian Army at that point in time. 'Operation Bluestar' in 1984 was successfully executed during his tenure as Army Chief.

I received a rail journey warrant from the regimental centre for my travel from the nearest railway station to Mumbai and back, along with an intimation about the officers' mess, where my accommodation arrangements were made in Mumbai.

As my written examinations were over, I travelled to Mumbai for the investiture ceremony with a relaxed mind. It was fun to be with the Army crowd once again for a few days.

The investiture parade was held at Shivaji Park, Dadar in Mumbai, where General Vaidya presented the medals to all recipients.

Receiving a prestigious gallantry award from the President through the Army Chief meant a lot to me, and that too in just over 5 years of Army service. Also known as 'decorations' in the Army, such awards are used as suffixes with the names of the awardee officers. In addition to being a great honour, the military decorations also come with many rewards and privileges for the awardees for life.

Chapter XIII

A Black Chapter

"Some goals are so worthy, it's glorious even to fail."
–Captain Manoj Kumar Pandey, PVC

"Why the hell are you not performing your duties?" I yelled at the Assistant Sub-Inspector (ASI) as I got down from the jeep with my gun in hand. Hurriedly getting up from his chair and trying to wear his beret, he came to attention. All the Constables around also did the same.

I knew fully well that as an ex-Army officer, I had no authority over a civilian police officer. Still, the situation was so charged up that I had no option but to shout at the plump ASI to remind him of his duties. Perhaps misled by my mannerisms, physique, and haircut, the ASI mistook me for a police officer in civvies.

The unruly crowd of a few hundred people was also taken by surprise. The crowd, gathered outside the Sher-e-Punjab Cloth Depot, pelting stones and shouting inflammatory slogans until a little while ago, suddenly went silent. In front of them, a few policemen who had been relaxing under a banyan tree a moment ago suddenly came to attention, which was something inexplicable to them.

Next to the scene was a double-storey building, on the ground floor of which was the Sher-e-Punjab Cloth Depot. The first floor of the building was the residence of Sardar Surjeet Singh, where he, along with his younger brother Rajinder Singh, a cousin of theirs and a few of his Sikh salesmen, resided. The police officer in charge, who had kept his eyes closed until a little while ago, was now instructing his men to control the crowd.

It was 2nd November 1984. While appearing for my UPSC Civil Services Examinations, I was preparing for my last paper, scheduled to be held on 6th November. Earlier in the afternoon of 31st October, when I was busy with my preparations, I heard the news of the assassination of the then Prime Minister, Indira Gandhi. In the following 2-3 days, the country witnessed widespread violence and arson.

The news of widespread violence in Delhi and many other cities poured in on 1st November. Highly provocative statements and conduct by a few political leaders resulted in the deterioration of the situation, and many places witnessed the unfortunate killing of thousands of innocent people. The violence escalated on 2nd November, and many affected areas were either brought under curfew or under prohibitory orders issued under Section 144 of the CrPC.

The peaceful state of Himachal Pradesh, including my native town of Bilaspur, was no exception. Late in the morning of Friday, 2nd November, I got a phone call from my wife from her bank branch, which was a few hundred metres away from Sher-e-Punjab Cloth Depot.

"Suno, a mob has attacked the house-cum-shop of Surjeet Singh Bhai Sa'ab. They are pelting stones and one of his salesmen is being beaten up,' I heard her say hurriedly, with a sense of urgency in her voice.

"All others are holed up inside the house. The situation is alarming, and the unruly crowd can do anything. Can we do something to save them?" She uttered the above sentences in one breath.

"Aren't any policemen around?" Alarmed, I asked her.

"Yes, there are a few," Shashi replied, "But they are mere spectators."

Surjeet Singh was a close family friend running a booming retail cloth business there. Originally from the Amritsar District of Punjab, he had established his business in Bilaspur about 12 years ago and had virtually monopolised the entire cloth business in the town by offering good quality cloth at affordable prices. Though his family and parents were in Amritsar, he lived in Bilaspur.

Surjeet's shop was just across my father's shop on a main crossing in the main market. He was very affable, treating me and my younger brother like his own brothers and respecting my father as his own. Taking due precaution, prohibitory orders were issued by the DM and most of the shops in the market were closed.

Despite imposing Section 144 of CrPC in the town, the banks were open. Shashi's workplace was in another building nearby, where the entire area was visible. Shashi could see the mob outside Surjeet's shop and also the brutal thrashing of one of his sales boys, who had gone out to get something from the market.

The phone call perturbed me, and I replied, "I will get back to you in a moment."

While placing the receiver back on the cradle, I pondered over the issue. How could the madness engulf the people even in a small town which virtually had no history of any communal violence ever? The Hindus and minuscule minorities like the Muslims, the Sikhs, and a few Christians had been living there in complete harmony for decades.

I remembered my school and college days there when my Muslim and Sikh friends would celebrate Hindu festivals like Holi, Dussehra, and Diwali with more enthusiasm than many of us. Granthi of the Gurudwara and Maulvi of the Masjid were friends to many prominent persons in the Hindu community. And all of a sudden, how come this communal frenzy?

My immediate reaction was to call the Superintendent of Police. A gentleman, perhaps his PA, took the call.

"Put me through to the SP," I said firmly.

"Who is speaking, sir?" asked the man on the other side.

"I am Captain Shekhar Gupta," I replied, with a sense of urgency.

"I am sorry, sir, but he is in a meeting with the District Magistrate. Kindly call again in about an hour. Do you want to leave any message for him, sir?" the man on the other end said politely.

"Yes, tell him that I am going to assume the responsibility of saving a few lives, which his machinery has miserably failed to do." Uttering these words sternly, I put the phone down.

Sensing no prompt solution from the Government agencies, I discussed the matter with my father and younger brother Suneel, telling them about Shashi's phone call. My mother also joined the discussion. The entire family, more particularly my father, had a very liberal outlook in such matters, and on many occasions, I found him to be much ahead of his time in his socio-religious approach.

"What do you propose?" he asked me.

"For their safety, please allow them to be kept at our house until the situation improves," I requested firmly. "If you permit, I, along with Suneel, will go rescue them all and bring them here for a few days."

"I am glad that you suggested it," my father said. "Even if Surjeet were not a close friend, I would still have asked you to do so on humanitarian grounds. Both of you, please go ahead." My mother and brother also nodded in agreement.

Those days, owning a four-wheeler was a luxury that we could ill afford. One of our cousins owned a second-hand jeep bought from Army disposal, and my brother requested him over the phone to lend the jeep to us for a while. As he agreed, my brother quickly went to his place in the neighbourhood and drove the jeep to the main gate of our house.

In the meantime, I tried calling Surjeet but could not get through. I quickly took out my licensed gun and loaded both its barrels. I also stuffed a few extra cartridges in my pocket.

As we both left, my father informed my wife over the phone that we were on the way. The open jeep with a gun in my hands caught the eye of all those we came across on a 2-kilometre road to Surjeet's house. Carrying a licensed gun in an area where prohibitory orders are enforced is illegal, but under the situation, there seemed to be no other option.

As we approached the scene, we stopped the jeep at a distance and observed the area from a vantage point. I could see a mob of around 300 people outside Surjeet's house pelting stones and shouting provocative slogans. After considering the situation for a few seconds, we moved the vehicle closer.

As my brother stopped the jeep near the scene, I could see a police detachment, oblivious to the happenings around them, relaxing on chairs in the shade of a banyan tree. I got out of the vehicle with my gun and moved straight towards the policemen. My brother accompanied me.

❧ ❧ ❧

With the police detachments getting active and trying to rein in the crowd, we swiftly entered the building from the backyard. The crowd seemed a bit confused, though many could perhaps recognise us.

We climbed up the stairs and knocked on the door. Surjeet and others had already seen the jeep and were waiting for us. To my surprise, the wife of Surjeet's cousin, who appeared to be in an advanced stage of pregnancy, was also there. They quickly packed a couple of small bags, and in 2-3 minutes, we all came out of the house and proceeded towards the jeep.

On their toes now, the police personnel were successful in keeping the crowd under control. There was some slogan shouting by the mob on seeing us all, but the police seemed to be in control. I made the lady sit in the front seat, and all seven of us huddled up at the back of the open jeep. As Suneel turned the jeep back, I saw my wife and her colleagues standing outside the bank branch and watching the entire sequence.

With my gun still held high, my brother started driving us back home. But as the jeep sped away, we did hear louder slogans behind us.

Surjeet Singh broke down when he entered our house and expressed his gratitude for rescuing them all. He told us that the miscreants had snapped the wires of his landline phones, and the police present on the spot were not taking any action to protect them. My father reassured Surjeet that they were all safe with us. My mother had kept two rooms ready for them, with a few beds and mattresses, with some bedding on the floor.

But there was much more to follow. The same day, at around 2.30 pm, I got another phone call from Shashi. She asked me to come to her bank branch to pick up one Tejinder Singh Sudan roughed up badly by a few hooligans. My wife also informed me that when Sudan went to his rented flat during the lunch break, 3-4 people attacked him, inflicting some injuries on him. After the incident, he felt insecure at his flat and asked my wife if he could stay at our house until normalcy was restored.

Sudan was a Sikh colleague of hers who had come on transfer from Delhi a few months ago and was living there alone.

I informed my father and went to the bank branch on Suneel's scooter. Sudan's face had some bruises visible, and one of his eyes had turned dark and was badly swollen. Sudan seemed badly shaken by the incident and eagerly waited for me with a small handbag in his hand. A few minutes later, Sudan also joined our family.

In the afternoon at around 16:30 hrs, I found my father speaking to someone over the phone. During the call, his face suddenly turned pale, and he seemed completely shaken. Guessing the nature of the call, I immediately snatched the receiver from his hands.

"Hello, who is it?" I bellowed into the mouthpiece.

"It is not important who I am," I could hear a cold voice.

The man on the other side continued in a threatening tone, "Listen to me carefully. If you don't throw all the *Sardars* out of your house today, you will have to repent."

"To hell with you! Do whatever you want," I shouted. "And tell me who you are," I asked, raising my voice again.

"If you do not throw the 'traitors' out of your house by this evening, we will set your cinema on fire," the caller on the other side continued in the same tone and tenor. "And we will also torch your house and shop."

"I am waiting for you with both barrels of my gun loaded. You dare, and carry your dead body on your own shoulders," I said firmly into the mouthpiece.

The line went dead. It could have been merely an intimidating and fake call, but a threat was conveyed nonetheless. Senseless passions were running high, and anything was possible. Given the situation, I could not afford to take such a threat lightly.

I discussed the entire scenario with my father and brother. My father was the chairperson of several institutions, including the Municipal Committee and District Beopar Mandal, and was well acquainted with the DM. I suggested to my father that the best course of action would be for him to speak to the District Magistrate (DM) and request some security.

He called the DM and informed him about the turn of events, including the threats. The DM was aware that we had rescued a few people and kept them at our residence. He immediately deployed a 6-man detachment of armed police to guard our residence around the clock, until further orders. Within an hour, the armed police personnel reported to our residence and took up positions near our main entrance gate. After that, no anonymous telephonic calls were received.

Later in the evening, the DM called my father again and informed him that our cinema hall and shop were already covered under an armed patrolling route. He also told my father that he had issued specific instructions to tighten the day and night surveillance around the above two areas.

At around 1830 hrs in the evening, my brother and I decided to take a round of the town to get a feel of the general sentiments.

Though many of the shops were closed, quite a few people were walking. To our surprise, many of our friends and cousins who met us on the way turned their faces away from us. It was saddening to note how senseless the people could turn with charged emotions against a particular community.

The parents and other family members of all those staying with us were concerned about their safety, particularly after the disturbing news from the national capital region. So that evening, all of them booked trunk calls and spoke to their families, informing them about their well-being and the safe harbour.

The communal hysteria, however, did not last long. Within a couple of days, many friends and relations who initially appeared to disapprove of our action either called us up or visited our house to express their solidarity with what we had done. A few of them also uttered a few words of appreciation for our action, perhaps to make up for their negative reaction earlier.

The next week was quite stressful for the entire family. In addition to the tension created by the threat, everyone was generally stressed out. More people used the facilities in the house than they were designed for. Particularly, the ladies in the house, i.e. my mother and wife, were hard-pressed with additional household chores. At the same time, everyone was pleased that God had chosen us for a once-in-a-lifetime opportunity to help a few fellow human beings under an exceptionally challenging situation.

After a few more days, the town limped back to normality. After being with our family for about eight days, Surjeet, his family members, his staff, and Sudan returned to their respective native places to meet their families. Soon thereafter, they returned to Bilaspur to resume their routine jobs.

What we did during the crisis was only our duty as responsible citizens. Over the last four decades, Surjeet and his brother Rajinder have repeatedly expressed their gratitude to us. After Sudan was transferred to New Delhi in 1985, we met him in Delhi after eighteen years, when in 2013, he invited us to his son's wedding. He fondly remembered the time spent at our house during those stressful days.

Surjeet, in particular, has not missed any opportunity since then to recollect the incident with profound gratitude whenever he meets us, specifically during family functions and social gatherings, and at times to the extent of embarrassing us by overdoing it. More particularly, he repeatedly thanks Shashi for promptly informing me about the unruly gathering outside his house that day; otherwise, extending any help to him wouldn't have been possible.

About a year ago, when I met Surjeet Singh during a social gathering, I told him about my intention to write this book. He asked me to include the above incident as well. Initially, I was a bit reluctant as the incident was outside the scope of this book, but it was on his insistence that I finally decided to include this chapter.

Fear is one of the most dominant emotions, and at times, fear of the unknown deters us from doing something right under a threatening situation. During this entire incident, our family was no exception, particularly after the telephonic call. But it was perhaps the exposure to the armed forces that prompted me not only to initiate the rescue effort along with my family but also to allay the fears of my family members after the threats.

To overcome the unknown fear in any situation has been one of the most important learnings imbibed by me during the six-year term in the Army. During those days full of anxiety, the entire family jointly derived moral strength from one another to accomplish the noble task under the trying circumstances.